MW00716936

Presented to:

_____

Presented by:

_____

Date:

_____

Product developed by Bordon Books, Tulsa, Oklahoma.
Concept: David Bordon and Tom Winters
Project Writing: Jeff Adams, Rebecca Currington, Mary Hake, and Michael Klassen in association with SnapdragonGroup[sm] Editorial Services.
Design by Greg Jackson, Thinkpen Design

FaithWords
Hachette Book Group USA
1271 Avenue of the Americas
New York, NY 10020

Visit our Web site at www.faithwords.com.

The FaithWords name and logo are trademarks of Hachette Book Group USA.

Printed in the United States of America
First Edition: August 2007
10 9 8 7 6 5 4 3 2 1
ISBN 10: 0-446-57939-4
ISBN 13: 978-0-446-57939-1

LCCN: 2006938652

Life's

SIMPLE GUIDE TO

GOD

Inspirational Insights for Growing Closer to God

David Bordon and Tom Winters

New York Boston Nashville

INTRODUCTION

If you're reading this book, you must be sensing a desire within yourself to know God better, to grow closer to Him, to learn more about His ways. That's a good thing, because you will never be in better company than when you are spending time in the presence of the One who created you, redeemed you, and loves you unfailingly.

The keys to growing closer to God are found in the Bible—God's true handbook for life—and this book, *Life's Simple Guide to God: Inspirational Insights for Growing Closer to God*, was designed to help you tap into the truths that can be found there. Of course, there is no end to what can be found in the Bible concerning your relationship with God, but we have pulled out some of the most practical truths, and we hope they will be a good beginning, an appropriate place to start as you pursue the true and living God.

CONTENTS

Life's

SIMPLE GUIDE TO

GOD

*Oh, the fullness, pleasure, sheer excitement
of knowing God on Earth!*

JIM ELLIOT

BE ON THE LOOKOUT FOR MIRACLES.

As they reached the place where the road started down from the Mount
of Olives, all of his followers began to shout and sing as they walked
along, praising God for all the wonderful miracles they had seen.

LUKE 19:37 NLT

Thousands of people followed Jesus through the Galilean
countryside. They were captivated by His persona, intrigued by
His teaching, but mostly, they were there to see the miracles.
They were generously rewarded for their effort: before their
eyes, they saw the deaf hear, the blind regain their sight, the
lame walk, the possessed delivered, the sick healed, and the
dead raised. They also saw lives miraculously changed: rugged
fishermen transformed into ministers of God's mercy and grace,
a dishonest tax collector who refunded all he had stolen, and a
prostitute whose newfound devotion to God was publicly praised
by Jesus Himself.

For those who are willing to follow Christ, there are daily
miracles still to be seen—miracles of provision, intervention,
protection, healing, transformation, and deliverance. They are
not confined to a certain place or time. Today, miracles can be
found wherever people are looking for them—in their communi-
ties, their homes, and their hearts.

Keep your eyes open for miracles and you will find yourself closer to God, because miracles follow the Master wherever He goes. They are the signs of His divine authority and compassion and the unmistakable manifestation of His presence in our lives. And if you should wake one morning to find that you need a miracle, you'll be in a perfect position to receive one.

SIMPLY SPEAKING

A miracle in the sense of the New Testament is not so much a breach of the laws of nature, but rather a remarkable or exceptional occurrence which brought an undeniable sense of the presence and power of God.

CHARLES DODD

☺ LIVING THE GOD LIFE

What miracle, small or large, have you seen God perform recently? Be sure to thank Him for the daily miracles He brings into your life.

ADJUST YOUR PRIORITIES.

[Jesus said,] Put God's kingdom first. Do what he wants you to do.
Then all of those things will also be given to you.

MATTHEW 6:33 NIRV

Jesus was a busy man. He healed sick people and fed the hungry. He taught those willing to listen; He tried to teach the religious leaders. He restored sanity to the insane. He went to church, read, and studied the Scriptures. He prayed for others and He spent time alone.

At times, Jesus needed a break from the demands on His life. On one occasion, after an exhausting day, He sent His disciples across a lake to another town. Instead of going with them, He told them He'd catch up later and went to the mountains to pray.

Jesus needed to know what to do. He gathered His thoughts and cleared His mind so He could hear God's answers. Jesus knew that His power came from spending time with God—so He made that His top priority.

You're busy too: soccer practice, music lessons, dance, gymnastics. That report needs to be on your boss's desk by noon tomorrow. Pay the bills, buy the groceries, get gas for the car, pick up the dry cleaning. Don't forget a card, flowers, dinner, and a movie for your anniversary. Oh, and lunch with your mom on her birthday. There never seems to be enough time for all you need to do.

Do as Jesus did: run to your heavenly Father. If you don't know what to say—say nothing, just sit in His presence. It's there that you'll receive the power you need to face each new day as you continue to manage your responsibilities appropriately and serve others with patience and love.

SIMPLY SPEAKING

When you put God first, you are establishing order for everything else in your life.

ANDREA GARNEY

☺ LIVING THE GOD LIFE

It's time for a priority check! What things have been taking up much of your time recently? What things do you need to spend more time on? How can you bring balance between these two?

LET GO OF SELF.

[Jesus said,] If you love your life, you will lose it. If you give it up in this world, you will be given eternal life.

JOHN 12:25 CEV

While He was here on earth, Jesus said some curious things. For example:

- "Blessed are you when people insult you, persecute you and falsely say all kinds of evil against you because of me. Rejoice and be glad" (Matthew 5:11–12).
- "Do not worry about your life, what you will eat or drink; or about your body, what you will wear" (Matthew 6:25).
- "Whoever wants to save his life will lose it, but whoever loses his life for me will find it" (Matthew 16:25).
- "Anyone who will not receive the kingdom of God like a little child will never enter it" (Luke 18:17).
- "If anyone wants to be first, he must be the very last, and the servant of all" (Mark 9:35).

Jesus often talked about self-sacrifice. He told one rich young man to sell everything he owned and give the money to the poor. He told His disciples to give up their businesses and follow Him with no hint of what was to come.

These statements seem odd because they are all promoting

the idea that we are to renounce self and life for God. The more we focus on our own thoughts, our own ambitions, our own interests, the more we move away from God.

Just like the people who followed Jesus through the countryside and wondered at His words, you must also choose to put others above yourself. It's the key to living each day close to God.

SIMPLY SPEAKING

God first, others second, self last.

AUTHOR UNKNOWN

☺ LIVING THE GOD LIFE

What have you done lately for someone other than yourself?

GIVE UP YOUR GRUDGES.

*[Jesus said,] When you are praying, first forgive anyone
you are holding a grudge against, so that your Father in heaven
will forgive your sins, too.*

MARK 11:25 NLT

Jesus was a forgiver—He still is!

He forgave a woman caught in bed with a man who wasn't
her husband. Instead of siding with the religious leaders who
wanted to kill her, He told her, "I don't condemn you. Don't do it
again." Another woman, presumably a career prostitute, poured
expensive perfume on Jesus' feet at a dinner held by a Pharisee
named Simon. Jesus told Simon that although the woman's sins
were numerous, He forgave her for everything she'd done.

Jesus pardoned Zacchaeus, a tax collector, for cheating
people. He forgave Peter when he said, "I don't know Him." He
absolved the rest of the disciples for deserting Him in the Garden
of Gethsemane when He asked them to pray. He forgave Thomas
when he doubted Jesus' resurrection.

Maybe the most dramatic act of forgiveness came when Jesus
looked down from the cross and forgave His tormentors and
executioners. Though He carried His cross, He refused to carry a
grudge.

If you want to be closer to God, you must forgive as well—no matter how deeply you've been hurt or offended. Your unfaithful spouse, your rebellious child, your abusive parent, your inconsiderate neighbor, the man or woman who made you a victim of crime: these people have earned your anger and hatred. But if it was possible for Jesus to forgive what was done to Him, it must be possible for you as well. If He laid down His grudges and forgave, then it must also be the right thing for you to do.

Take those grudges and throw them into the sea of forgetfulness. Once you do, you can begin to heal, and you'll find yourself able to hear God's voice—tender and caring—calling you to draw close.

SIMPLY SPEAKING 📣
To carry a grudge is like being stung to death by one bee.
WILLIAM H. WALTON

☺ LIVING THE GOD LIFE

*W*hom do you need to forgive today? Do it.

KEEP YOUR EYES ON JESUS.

[God said,] I will not in any way fail you nor give you up nor leave you
without support. [I will] not, [I will] not, [I will] not in any degree leave
you helpless nor forsake nor let [you] down (relax My hold on you)!
[Assuredly not!]

HEBREWS 13:5 AMP

It's not always easy to keep your eyes on Jesus. Peter had that
problem when he and the other disciples spent a night in the
middle of a storm at sea.

After meeting people's needs all day, Jesus sent the disciples
on ahead to the next city He wanted to visit. To get there, they
had to cross the Sea of Galilee. So the former fisherman and
others got in a boat and set out on what should have been a short
trip. It wasn't.

The clouds gathered, the winds picked up, and darkness fell.
The disciples rowed harder and harder, but they didn't make
much progress. At some point during the night, in the midst of
their struggle, they thought they saw a ghost. But Peter thought
he recognized the man and called out, "Jesus! Is that You? If it's
really You, tell me to come."

"Get out of the boat, Peter. It's Me." At the worst possible
time, Jesus asked Peter to trust Him. He didn't ask him to do the

impossible—to walk on water. Jesus asked Peter to do the one thing Peter could do—abandon the boat and come to Him.

It's not easy to leave your security behind—even when it's foundering. But when circumstances threaten to overwhelm you, the safest place to be is walking above your troubles with your eyes on Jesus. Even if you look down as Peter did and begin to sink, Jesus will pull you to safety.

SIMPLY SPEAKING

Faith is deliberate confidence in the character of God whose ways you may not understand at the time.

OSWALD CHAMBERS

☺ LIVING THE GOD LIFE

What area of your life is God especially asking you to trust Him with right now?

PRACTICE MORE WALK, LESS TALK.

Don't just listen to the word. You fool yourselves if you do that. You must do what it says.

JAMES 1:22 NIRV

Our words matter—there is no doubt about that. They are powerful and God uses them all the time to comfort, encourage, educate, clarify, and build up others. Your words can show someone the way to God—or back to Him. But words alone are not enough.

Every day the people around you watch your life, wondering if your words are proven in it. Do you walk in the truths you expound to others? Do you urge others to pray but make it a low priority in your own life? Do you encourage others to be strong and trust God while you carry around an attitude of defeat? Do you teach that we are to love each other while neglecting to show love to people in your life?

To be close to God, we must be honest with ourselves, routing out the hypocrisy and the sin that lingers in our hearts. But once we begin to walk our talk, our lives become powerful examples of God's grace and mercy.

Most of the New Testament is filled with the words of the apostle Paul. He had a lot to say about almost every aspect of living in relationship with God. And his words were often difficult to hear, urging repentance, sacrifice, discipline, and humility—just for starters. Paul's words were effective, however, because he walked his talk on every level. He never asked others to do anything that he was not already doing.

Take a look at your words and see if they are in harmony with your life. If they aren't, ask God to help you walk in His truth before those who hear your good message of hope and redemption and victory.

SIMPLY SPEAKING

Gladly we desire to make other men perfect,
but we will not amend our own fault.

THOMAS À KEMPIS

☺ LIVING THE GOD LIFE

*D*oes the walk you walk match the talk you talk? In what ways can you better live out your Christian faith?

OBEY GOD'S RULES OF RIGHT LIVING.

[Jesus said,] If you love me, you will obey my commandments.

JOHN 14:15 GNB

Jesus told a story about a man who had two sons. The older one obeyed their father; the younger one didn't. He wanted to live life by his own rules. But he hadn't learned what he needed to know.

He asked his father for his inheritance, his portion of the estate. So his dad gave him what he wanted.

Soon afterward, the young man left for a place far away from home. He made bad choices in his life. He partied, gambled, and slept with promiscuous women. In the end, he had nothing—not even enough for his next meal.

Homeless and hopeless, he got a job, the worst one he could get—slopping hogs. Hungry himself, he fed pigs, but his boss wouldn't let him eat the animals' food.

All the while, at home, his brother worked.

When the younger son realized his dad's hired hands had plenty of food to eat, he decided to go home.

His dad saw him, ran to meet him, and threw a party in his honor. The older brother complained, "I've done everything you asked and more, but you've given me nothing."

"All I have is yours," his father said.

The son didn't understand that his obedience paid off.

Maybe you think God rewards the disobedience of others rather than your hard work. He doesn't, but it's easy to feel resentment.

You forget that everything your Father has is already yours. Instead of complaining, do what the older brother didn't do—celebrate. And remember that when you're bad, you can come home, and that obedience pays rich dividends you may not know are yours.

SIMPLY SPEAKING

It has been well remarked, it is not said that after keeping God's commandments, but in keeping them there is great reward. God has linked these two things together, and no man can separate them—obedience and peace.

FREDERICK WILLIAM ROBERTSON

☺ LIVING THE GOD LIFE

Thank God today that He richly rewards your obedience—even in unexpected ways!

GO IN SEARCH OF GOD'S PURPOSE FOR YOUR LIFE.

We are God's masterpiece. He has created us anew in Christ Jesus, so that we can do the good things he planned for us long ago.

EPHESIANS 2:10 NLT

When Jesus called His disciples, they didn't know what to expect.

He told Peter and John, "Leave your boats and nets; stop fishing; I'll teach you to catch men."

All of the disciples left their normal lives and followed Jesus. For three years they lived with Him. They watched what He did, listened to what He taught, performed miracles themselves, and perhaps began to believe they could accomplish almost anything.

Their motives are unknown, but maybe they wanted their lives to count for something. Perhaps these men hoped they could make a difference, at least in their small towns. It seems certain they had no idea that when they followed Jesus, they would discover their destinies, but they did.

Forty days after Jesus rose from the dead, the once-cowardly Peter preached one sermon that revolutionized the lives of more than three thousand people. And John watched how the world will end and wrote about it for the sake of those of us who would come later.

These men had no way of knowing how important their contributions would be. That's what makes God's plan so amazing. He always does more than we ever expected, more than we ever dreamed.

Are you ready to lay down your "nets," to follow Jesus wherever He leads? If so, you're in for the sweet communion of sharing each day with the Lord and the privilege of living a great adventure with eternal reward.

SIMPLY SPEAKING 📢

Live as with God; and whatever be your calling,
pray for the gift that will perfectly qualify
you in it.

HORACE BUSHNELL

🙂 LIVING THE GOD LIFE

What is Jesus calling you to do with your life? What is it that makes you come alive?

HUMBLE YOURSELF.

[Jesus said,] Everyone who exalts himself will be humbled, and he who humbles himself will be exalted.

LUKE 14:11

John the Baptist was at the top of his game. The most popular preacher of his day, he drew bigger crowds than the jealous religious leaders. Multitudes came to hear him preach. There were no buildings big enough to accommodate the crowds, so he held his meetings alfresco. His reputation grew continually, even without the help of radio broadcasts, television shows, a Web site, or podcasts.

Success can make people believe they're more important than they are and neglect to credit God for His role in their achievements. Success can lead to crisis.

John faced such a dilemma: move up or move on. The time came for Jesus to take center stage and for John to exit. John chose to do the right thing: "I must become less important—because I am; He must become more important—because He is."

When you're successful, it's easy to think you got where you are because you're smart. It's easy to forget what God did, how He helped you.

It's also easy to forget that not everyone agrees with your

opinion of yourself. It's hard, at times, to look in the mirror and face the truth. But when you do—when you humble yourself as John did—you'll like what you see: a reflection of Jesus.

SIMPLY SPEAKING

True humility is not an abject, groveling, self-despising spirit; it is but a right estimate of ourselves as God sees us.

TRYON EDWARDS

☺ LIVING THE GOD LIFE

Humility is often a hard lesson to learn, but it reaps great rewards. How can you make Jesus greater in your life— and make yourself smaller?

GIVE FREELY OF WHAT YOU HAVE.

The generous prosper and are satisfied; those who refresh others will
themselves be refreshed.

PROVERBS 11:25 NLT

The life of Jesus was a life of giving. He healed the sick, fed
the hungry, restored hope to the hopeless, and handed out
a countless number of second chances. Though He had little
money, He was generous—lavishly so—with those in need.

More than once, Jesus healed lepers, returning to them both
their health and their acceptance in the community. He gave
sweet peace to the demoniac, who lived—until Jesus freed him—
a life of torment and despair. He generously returned a son to
his grieving mother and a daughter to her desperate centurion
father. He gave these people what they needed most and could
not obtain for themselves. And He gave without thought of
reciprocation.

Are you willing to be that kind of giver, the God kind?
The Bible teaches that by the Holy Spirit's power in your life,
you can be that kind of giver too! You can be generous in
your prayers, your words of encouragement, and your smiles.
You can give of your time by offering to babysit for a frazzled
mother or mow your elderly neighbor's lawn. And you can

share what you have of a material nature as God leads you.

As you learn to give as God gives, you will be sharing His heart of compassion and love for hurting, struggling humanity. It's hard to imagine being any closer to God than that.

SIMPLY SPEAKING 📣

For the Macedonian Christians, giving was not a chore but a challenge, not a burden but a blessing. Giving was not something to be avoided, but a privilege to be desired.

GEORGE SWEETING

☺ LIVING THE GOD LIFE

To whom can you be a generous giver today?

LET GO OF WORRY.

[Jesus said,] Do not worry about tomorrow, for tomorrow will worry about itself. Each day has enough trouble of its own.

MATTHEW 6:34

A crowd of more than five thousand men, in addition to women and children, had been following Jesus and His disciples through the countryside. So focused were they on the words of life Jesus was speaking that they refused to break away to look for food. Then they were hungry, especially the little ones. When one of the disciples pointed this out to Jesus, He answered with only two words: "Feed them."

"With what?" they asked. "We don't have enough food for all of these people."

This must have been an anxious moment for the disciples, but not for Jesus. He pointed to a young boy who had just offered to share his lunch, five loaves of bread and two fish. He prayed, thanked God for what He had, and told His disciples to distribute the food and let the people take all they wanted. A short time later, everyone had been fed and the disciples gathered twelve baskets of leftovers.

You may be looking at what you have and wondering how it will ever be enough to meet your needs. Like Jesus' disciples, you may be worried, but your need can never be greater than your Supplier.

Whatever shortfalls you face, if you'll bring what little you have, God will multiply that until it's more than enough to meet your needs.

God doesn't want you to worry. Instead He wants you to trust Him, even when the outcome seems most uncertain. He'll never fail to provide for you.

SIMPLY SPEAKING 📢

There is no need too great for God.
He has unlimited resources at His disposal,
and He delights in making them available
to His children.

MERIWETHER WILLIAMS

☺ LIVING THE GOD LIFE

Start a "worry-buster" journal. Keep track of your needs and worries, but also record each time God provides for you, proving your worries illegitimate. You'll look back later and see a pattern of God's amazing faithfulness!

GET SERIOUS ABOUT LAUGHTER.

A cheerful disposition is good for your health;
gloom and doom leave you bone-tired.

PROVERBS 17:22 MSG

Many people have a perception of God as the sober
inhabitant of some beautiful but austere cathedral. Someone to
be in awe of—certainly. Someone to be respectful of—without
doubt. Someone to laugh with—well, not so much. But when you
look into God's Word, you may be surprised to find God deeply
invested in the lighter side of life.

Consider this: the word *rejoice*, in various tense forms,
appears in the New International Version of the Bible an
amazing 181 times. The word *joy* is mentioned even more—218
times. The word *joyful* adds 16 to the total number, leaving the
word *repent* in the dust at 39 appearances and the word *judgment*
with 132 mentions. The word *sober* is mentioned only twice.

In addition, the word *rejoice* is quite often used as a
command: "Rejoice in the Lord always. I will say it again:
Rejoice!" (Phil. 4:4). Or this passage from the book of Revelation:
"Our Lord God Almighty reigns. Let us rejoice and be glad and
give him glory!" (Rev. 19:6–7).

It would seem clear that our God is not a Glummy Gus who

likes to break up our fun and subdue our laughter. Rather He appears to be a God who encourages joyous outbursts of all kinds. Perhaps it's because He knows even better than we that we have a great deal to be happy about.

The next time you laugh, imagine God laughing with you. You were created in His image and you enjoy laughing. So, as inconceivable as it may seem, so does He!

SIMPLY SPEAKING

It is the soul that is not yet sure of its God that is afraid to laugh in His presence.

GEORGE MacDONALD

☺ LIVING THE GOD LIFE

*D*on't take life so seriously. Be willing to laugh at yourself, laugh with others, and laugh with God.

PRAY FOR THOSE WHO CURSE YOU.

[Jesus said,] You have heard that it was said, "Love your neighbor and hate your enemy." But I tell you: Love your enemies and pray for those who persecute you, that you may be sons of your Father in heaven.

MATTHEW 5:43–45

Throughout human history, the prevailing standard has been: get your enemies before they get you. If people hurt you, hurt them back—in the same way, to the same degree. Revenge is sweet. Then Jesus came along and turned that philosophy upside down by telling His disciples to love their enemies and pray for those who were persecuting them. Even today those words cut against the grain. Why would we be good to those who curse us and treat us badly?

Those who would be close to God must learn a new law, a law that supersedes all the others: the law of love. This law was set in place when Jesus gave His life for those who rejected and cursed Him. It broke the bitter cycle of hatred and revenge, an eye for an eye and a tooth for a tooth, and replaced it with a new cycle of forgiveness and reconciliation. Jesus' act of love toward those who abused Him reconciled us to our Creator, our heavenly Father.

Your human nature won't want to heed these words. It will

put up a struggle for sure. But with the help of God's Holy Spirit, you are capable of doing what Jesus did. You can look past the hateful stares, the alienating words, the hurtful actions. You can respond with blessing, with prayer, with kindness, and when you do, you will feel yourself drawing closer to God.

Not everyone will receive your love offering. But the benefit is not dependent upon the response, only on God's grace and goodness in your own life.

SIMPLY SPEAKING

He who returns a good for evil
obtains the victory.

THOMAS FULLER

☺ LIVING THE GOD LIFE

How can you begin to pray for the "enemies" in your life? What can you do to surprise them with an unexpected blessing?

READ THE BIBLE EACH DAY.

*All Scripture is inspired by God and is useful to teach us what is true
and to make us realize what is wrong in our lives. It straightens us out
and teaches us to do what is right.*

2 TIMOTHY 3:16 NLT

You could not miss many meals without the lack of food
affecting your physical vitality. In like manner, you need
sustenance to grow and thrive spiritually. God's Word provides
the nutrients necessary for a healthy spiritual life.

Reading the Bible feeds your spirit. God has provided His
Word in written form so all people might be able to know
Him better and learn how to live for Him. Unless you commit
to knowing God's Word, you will not fully experience God
Himself.

Before you begin to read or study Scripture, ask God to open
your mind to His truth and help you apply it to your life. He will
speak to you through His Word. God has promised His Word
will not return to Him empty but will prosper, accomplishing His
purposes in the lives of those who receive it. (See Isa. 55:11.)

God's holy Word is living and powerful. From His Book
you learn God's principles and how to live righteously. The
Scriptures can also admonish you, showing you any error in your

life and how to correct it. His Word brings comfort, hope, and wisdom and fills your heart with joy and peace.

The Bible is part of the believer's spiritual armor, called by Paul the "sword of the Spirit" (Eph. 6:17). Use it in battle against the devil, just as Jesus quoted it when Satan tempted Him.

Daily mine the treasures of God's Word, not just for your own knowledge, but to equip you to do good and share God's truth with others. The Bible contains the answers to life's problems and points the way to heaven. Plan to read through the entire Bible. This will give you a complete picture of His interaction with mankind.

Crave God's Word as an infant desires milk. It is spiritual food you cannot do without.

SIMPLY SPEAKING

The Bible is God's chart for you to steer by, to keep you from the bottom of the sea, and to show you where the harbor is, and how to reach it without running on rocks and bars.

HENRY WARD BEECHER

☺ **LIVING THE GOD LIFE**

*W*hy not start a new Bible reading plan—one that is easy to incorporate into your daily life but one that also draws you deeper into the study of God's Word? It will be an investment of your time that you will never regret.

BE AT PEACE.

[Jesus said,] I give you peace, the kind of peace that only I can give.
It isn't like the peace that this world can give.
So don't be worried or afraid.

JOHN 14:27 CEV

Peace is hard to come by these days. In many parts of
the world, war rages. People blow themselves up just to kill
others. Ancient feuds continue between groups who hate each
other because that's what they've done as long as anyone can
remember. But peace isn't just the absence of conflict. It is a state
of mind, a condition of the heart that comes only when we make
room for God in our lives.

Joseph and Mary traveled from Nazareth to their hometown
to register in a census as ordered by the Roman government.
The trip by donkey took days. They couldn't call ahead for hotel
reservations, so by the time they arrived, "No Vacancy" signs
hung everywhere.

Joseph asked one owner for a room. "Sorry, I don't have any
left." All that was available was the stable. Desperate, with Mary
in labor, Joseph agreed to accommodations in a smelly barn full
of animals.

That night the Prince of Peace came to Earth, but the too-busy, nearly exhausted world didn't notice. God filled the sky with angels to get the attention of a few sleepy shepherds. They believed enough to leave their sheep—not what shepherds normally do—but they were the only ones.

If your stomach is churning and you long for peace, perhaps you need to make room for the Prince of Peace in your life. Invite Him to be the very center, the focal point of your activities. Speak to Him often, even if that means leaving your "sheep" for a short time in order to spend time getting to know Him.

Only as you grow closer to God will you finally be at peace.

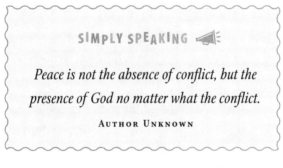

SIMPLY SPEAKING

Peace is not the absence of conflict, but the presence of God no matter what the conflict.

AUTHOR UNKNOWN

☺ LIVING THE GOD LIFE

Are you tired, stressed, or frustrated? Or does the Prince of Peace reign in your heart? As you invite Him into your life, He will calm your anxious spirit and bring you His peace—which passes all understanding.

BE PATIENT WITH YOURSELF.

Love is patient.

1 CORINTHIANS 13:4 NIRV

Jesus chose twelve men to be His disciples. They were fisherman and tax collectors. He didn't expect them to understand complex spiritual truths overnight. He asked them only to follow.

The patient Teacher must have been pleased to hear Peter's answer to His question: "Who do you say I am?" Other people said Jesus was a great prophet or teacher, but Peter recognized that He was the Messiah. He said, "You are the Christ, the Son of the living God" (Matt. 16:15–16).

Peter was—as are we all—a human being, subject to moments of inspiration and spiritual insight, capable of loving God with all his heart, but fallible, imperfect. He followed his great statement of faith and fact by denying three times that he even knew Jesus. After His resurrection, Jesus made it a point to forgive Peter. He knew Peter was growing, still becoming the man He created him to be.

Do you long to be close to God—closer than you've ever been before? Are you trying to do everything right, everything you can possibly do to please Him, to gain His approval? Relax.

You already have it. All He asks is that you follow. You'll have moments of glorious insight as well as grievous missteps along the way, but you'll get there, just as Peter did. A few months after Jesus' resurrection Peter preached to thousands of people in Jerusalem. His words were so powerful that a great number became Christians. You will do great things in your future as well, as long as you allow yourself time to grow.

SIMPLY SPEAKING

Be not afraid of growing slowly;
be afraid only of standing still.

CHINESE PROVERB

😊 LIVING THE GOD LIFE

Never underestimate your potential. God has a lot invested in you. And what He has started, He will finish.

LIGHTEN YOUR LOAD.

[Jesus said,] Come to me, all you who are weary and burdened,
and I will give you rest.

MATTHEW 11:28

In Jesus' time, the Pharisees and other religious
leaders emphasized keeping God's laws: not just the Ten
Commandments, but also every nuance of men's interpre-
tations of those rules for life. It's difficult enough to try
to keep ten, but imagine trying to remember—much less
obey—hundreds of regulations. Jesus pointed out that even
the leaders couldn't do it.

On one occasion, Jesus said to His followers: "Are you tired?
Worn out? Burned out on religion? Come to me. Get away with
me and you'll recover your life. I'll show you how to take a real
rest. Walk with me and work with me—watch how I do it. Learn
the unforced rhythms of grace. I won't lay anything heavy or
ill-fitting on you. Keep company with me and you'll learn to live
freely and lightly" (Matt. 11:28–30 MSG).

Keeping rules is hard; getting to know God isn't. Man makes
heavy what God intended to be light. And there's an even bigger
problem: you might carry your religious baggage all the way to
the end of your journey, stumbling, sweating, laboring with every

step, only to find when you get it there that it was all for nothing.

If you're carrying too many burdens—even if they seem to be good and noble—lighten your load. As you pray and seek Him, He will show you which ones you can lay down for good. Then He will help you carry the rest, lightening your load even more with His shared strength.

SIMPLY SPEAKING

Only the man who follows the command of Jesus single-mindedly and unresistingly lets his yoke rest upon him, finds his burden easy, and under its gentle pressure receives the power to persevere in the right way.

DIETRICH BONHOEFFER

☺ LIVING THE GOD LIFE

What are some burdens that you need to let go of in order to experience the joy of God's grace?

OPEN YOUR HEART.

*[Jesus said,] Listen! I am standing and knocking at your door. If you
hear my voice and open the door, I will come in.*

REVELATION 3:20 CEV

Over the three years of His public ministry, Jesus slept where
He could and occasionally ate with others who invited Him to
share a meal. These people were blessed because they opened
their homes. Others received much more—these opened their
homes to Him as well, but they also opened their hearts.

One family in Bethany—two sisters and one brother—
welcomed Jesus as often as possible. Jesus taught in their home
and ate with them. He stayed often and long enough that they
became good friends.

The day came when this family needed a miracle. The
brother fell ill. The sisters sent a message to Jesus and expected
Him to come quickly and heal him, but He did not arrive as
expected. By the time Jesus did come, Lazarus had been dead
for four days. How the sisters must have grieved as they gently
wrapped him in the burial cloth and watched as he was carried
to the tomb. "If only Jesus had been here . . ." they must have
whispered. But this story doesn't end as you might imagine.

When Jesus arrived, He found the sisters grieving, but their hearts were still open to Him. That day, Jesus raised their brother from the dead.

Have you opened your heart to God? Do you trust Him completely, no matter what circumstances you are facing in your life? When your heart is open, your life is open for a miracle.

SIMPLY SPEAKING 📢

You have trusted Him in a few things, and He has not failed you. Trust Him now for everything, and see if He does not do for you exceeding abundantly above all that you could ever have asked.

HANNAH WHITALL SMITH

☺ LIVING THE GOD LIFE

How open is your heart to the Lord? Why not write a prayer to Him today expressing your love and trust in Him?

TRAVEL LIGHT.

[Jesus said,] Don't hoard treasure down here where it gets eaten by moths and corroded by rust or—worse!—stolen by burglars. Stockpile treasure in heaven, where it's safe from moth and rust and burglars.

MATTHEW 6:19–20 MSG

A wealthy young ruler came to Jesus with a question: "What will happen to me when I die?" His education told him heaven was real, but he had no idea how to get there and no assurance that he would. He probably often took inventory of his behavior—trying to figure out what he needed to do to tip the scales in his favor. He tried to please God, but he had nagging doubts that the good he did would be enough to outweigh the bad.

He may have thought it difficult to win God's approval. Perhaps when he sinned, he envisioned an angry God. It probably seemed to him that he couldn't do enough.

When Jesus reminded him of the Ten Commandments—a good place to begin—he answered that he had carefully kept them his entire life. To this Jesus replied: "You still lack one thing. Sell everything you have and give to the poor, and you will have treasure in heaven. Then come, follow me" (Luke 18:22). The young ruler walked away saddened. He wanted to know God to receive eternal life—but he wanted his possessions more.

Maybe you're like him. You want to know God but there are too many things in the way. Don't walk away sad. Rid yourself of anything and everything that keeps you from following Him. One day your possessions will mean nothing. You will see that He is all that matters, all that ever mattered.

Travel light, and when you reach the end of your journey, you'll be able to face your eternal life with rejoicing rather than regret.

SIMPLY SPEAKING

I will place no value on anything I have or may possess, except in relation to the kingdom of Christ.

DAVID LIVINGSTONE

☺ LIVING THE GOD LIFE

What things are holding you back from experiencing a fuller, more satisfying relationship with God? Make a commitment to get rid of anything that hinders your relationship with Him.

COME CLEAN.

*If we confess our sins to God, he can always be trusted to forgive us
and take our sins away.*

1 JOHN 1:9 CEV

Since the beginning, there have been those who thought they
could grow close to God without coming clean with Him. This is
simply an impossibility. Though He knows us completely—every
flaw, every thought, every sin—He requires us to come to Him
with repentant hearts. What we do not acknowledge, He cannot
expunge. It lingers like ash in the air.

If you are serious about wanting to live in vital union with
God, loving Him, pleasing Him, communicating with Him
minute by minute, you must get honest with Him about any sin
He reveals to you.

No need to panic. God knows that full disclosure in one
horrifying moment would come close to killing us. As we come
before Him, willing to face those things that we've done wrong—
ungodly attitudes and behaviors, thoughts and speech—He will
help us identify, acknowledge, and put those things behind us.

In this world and perhaps even in heaven, you will not find
anything so invigorating, so life-giving, so joyful as a heart that
is clean before God. It's worth any sacrifice, any difficult work

of repentance, any discomfort. It is worth striving for with every ounce of your energy, every part of your being. For such a heart misses nothing but lives each day in constant communication with the Creator of the universe. Once you are aware of what you can have, why would you settle for anything less?

God is waiting for you. Don't hesitate. Open the stream of confession until only pure, clean water flows from within your soul.

SIMPLY SPEAKING

Confession is necessary for fellowship. Sin builds a barrier between us and God.

ERWIN W. LUTZER

☺ LIVING THE GOD LIFE

What do you need to acknowledge and confess to God today? Don't wait another minute—His forgiveness is ready and available right now!

LEARN A BETTER WAY.

The LORD is near to all who call on him,
to all who call on him in truth.

PSALM 145:18

Jesus said God cares more for His children than He does about plants and animals. Yet He takes care of the flowers and notices when even one bird dies. Jesus taught that people often underestimate their own worth.

Martha did that. On one occasion, Jesus and His disciples visited Martha and her sister, Mary. Mary sat at Jesus' feet while Martha prepared dinner. For Martha, that meant a five-star feast. After all, Jesus didn't visit everyone's home to enjoy a meal. An important man, Jesus deserved the best that could be offered. No expense should be spared; no detail should be overlooked. So Martha began her preparations.

Even though her guests arrived without warning, Martha arranged a banquet fit for a king. With a little help from Mary, the work would have been lighter. But she didn't get help from Mary, who sat in the living room listening to Jesus. That was the problem.

To Martha, it seemed that Mary had forgotten her responsibilities. But when she confronted Mary—in front of

Jesus—Martha learned what God deems important.

Martha complained to her guest of honor that Mary wasn't doing her fair share.

Jesus said, "Martha, you're working too hard. What you're doing isn't important. What Mary is doing is. Join us." (See Luke 10:38-42.)

Perhaps, like Martha, you often link your worth with your work. You think that you need to provide for God, when He wants to provide for you. That's an easy mistake to make and one that's easy to fix. Move your ministry, your church work, your newest spiritual project, or whatever, to a back burner for a few minutes and find a place at Jesus' feet. He is more interested in your company than your service.

SIMPLY SPEAKING 📣

In the rush and noise of life, as you have intervals, step home within yourselves and be still. Wait upon God, and feel his good presence; this will carry you evenly through your day's business.

WILLIAM PENN

🙂 LIVING THE GOD LIFE

Why not step aside from the hustle and bustle of daily life and spend some time at Jesus' feet today?

LOOK AROUND YOU.

By taking a long and thoughtful look at what God has created, people have always been able to see what their eyes as such can't see: eternal power, for instance, and the mystery of his divine being.

ROMANS 1:20 MSG

Have you ever watched a tiny, fluttering hummingbird drinking from a fuchsia's red blossoms? Or witnessed glittering diamonds decorating a dew-drenched spider's web at sunrise? Maybe you've been surprised by a brilliant rainbow emerging from a gray-clouded sky.

Consider the vastness of the oceans, which cover more than three-fourths of the earth. Observe the strength of a giant sequoia as your eyes follow its reddish-brown trunk up to its towering top. View rugged, snowcapped mountains stretching across the boundary between horizon and sky. Sense the power of a majestic waterfall as it splashes and careens down a rocky cliff. Stare at the star-studded night sky with its sparkling galaxies whirling through space. Notice colorful wildflowers brightening the banks along rural roads.

When you glimpse such scenic vistas, does awe rise within you? That sense of wonder tugging at your heart is more than just appreciation of nature's expansive beauty. This admiration of creation can lift you above yourself. If you allow it, it will draw your mind and heart to the Lord.

What response does God's handiwork evoke? When you enjoy a magnificent painting, you compliment the artist. Shouldn't you do the same for the Creator of the universe? As you look around at the world each day and survey the wonders of nature, take time to praise the Maker and Sustainer of all. In fact, you will be joining a mighty chorus—including the trees and the mountains and the hills—all praising the Creator.

As you revel with God amid the splendor of His creation, you will get to know Him more personally. Talk with Him about His world. He made it to share with you.

SIMPLY SPEAKING

I love to think of nature as an unlimited broadcasting station through which God speaks to us every hour, if we will only tune in.

GEORGE WASHINGTON CARVER

☺ LIVING THE GOD LIFE

Spend some time today in the magnificence of God's creation. Allow your heart to commune with your Creator as you bask in the grandeur of His world.

REPLACE FEAR WITH FAITH.

Everyone born of God overcomes the world.
This is the victory that has overcome the world, even our faith.

1 JOHN 5:4

Has fear kept you from trying something new? Have you allowed fears to rob you of friendships and fun? Could fear block your path toward success? Whether such fears are based on fact or phobia, they will hinder your life and growth.

How can you be set free from the bondage to fear?

God's key to releasing fear's prisoners is faith, which He freely supplies to all who ask. God not only says to the fearful, "Don't be afraid," He removes their fears. When Jesus' disciples trembled in a storm-battered boat, He calmed the wind and the waves. He will do the same for you.

When fear whispers words of worry and repeats, "What if?" refuse to listen to its attempts to terrorize. Suppose fears keep sneaking back to visit you. If you invite them in for a chat, you will find it difficult to get them to leave.

Ask the Lord to give you the faith you need to stand up and let your fears know that they are not welcome. Reading and meditating on God's Word will help your faith grow stronger. Faith is like a watchdog that will keep your fears at bay. If fears knock at your door, send faith to meet them, and they will slink away. Envision faith putting up signs that read, "Keep Out" and "No Fears Allowed."

Faith can always win the battle with fear. Believe it. Repeat it aloud. Live it out with confidence. You can't lose when you replace your fear with faith.

SIMPLY SPEAKING

There is much in the world to make us afraid.
There is much more in our faith to
make us unafraid.

FREDERICK W. CROPP

🙂 **LIVING THE GOD LIFE**

What are your greatest fears? Why not turn them over to God today, placing them in His capable hands and asking Him for the grace to overcome them in His strength?

BE AN ENCOURAGER.

Encourage one another and build each other up,
just as in fact you are doing.

1 THESSALONIANS 5:11

In Scripture, Barnabas serves as the epitome of encouragement. Without him, the early church may not have been as
successful, nor the New Testament as complete. Barnabas was
one of the first to sell what he owned and give the money to help
other Christians in Jerusalem. His reputation earned him the
nickname "Son of Encouragement," and he was even called an
apostle.

Barnabas took a risk to welcome Paul, a former persecutor,
into the church. Barnabas accompanied Paul on missionary trips
and encouraged new believers. When the two split over the issue
of John Mark, who had abandoned them on their first journey,
Barnabas took the young man along and encouraged him. Mark
developed into an effective minister and later traveled with Peter.
Mark wrote one of the gospels and Paul most of the epistles—
Bible material we might not have without Barnabas.

How can you, like Barnabas, encourage others?

- Be willing to take a risk, to sacrifice yourself in order to
  bless others.

- Share what you have with those in need—be it money, material goods, time, or expertise.
- Speak with young people about their lives and their futures, and listen to what they have to say.
- When people fall or fail, don't criticize them, but lift them up and come alongside to assist them on their way.
- Visit the elderly and the ill. Read to them or write letters for them.
- Tell your pastor how he has helped you.
- Compliment the grocery checker, the waiter, and other service personnel on their work.
- Send cards and notes expressing appreciation and encouragement.

Wouldn't you like to be known as an encourager? Become a Barnabas today.

SIMPLY SPEAKING

Many a time a word of praise or thanks or appreciation or cheer has kept a man on his feet. Blessed is the man who speaks such a word.

WILLIAM BARCLAY

☺ LIVING THE GOD LIFE

Who most needs your encouragement today? What will you do to become a "Barnabas" in his or her life?

SMILE INTO THE FACE OF GOD.

You have made known to me the path of life;
you will fill me with joy in your presence,
with eternal pleasures at your right hand.

PSALM 16:11

Smiles, like magnets, attract others and build bonds between people. As with people, so also with God. Smiling up at your heavenly Father draws you closer to Him. Your smiling face shows God you enjoy being in His presence. Smiling into His face expresses your appreciation for who He is. Smiles accompany a heart full of thanksgiving. Your smile reveals your love and delight in the relationship you share with God, even as it echoes His love and delight in you, His child.

You have no reason to hold back—you can be totally yourself with God. He already knows you inside and out, and He loves you intensely. So let your smile show your relief at His acceptance, your trust in His care, and your gratefulness for all He has done for you.

A simple smile can communicate so much. And God understands exactly what your heart is saying. No matter if you flash a timid smile when nervous or a goofy grin when you feel silly, God enjoys your smiles. The sacrifice of a smile offered to Him when you feel low will lift your spirits. No matter the situation, a smile to God will bless both the giver and the Receiver.

As your communion with the Lord grows sweeter and deeper, you will find your smile becomes such a natural part of your demeanor you don't even think about it. Others may wonder if you have a secret. But the secret behind your smile is not one you wish to keep to yourself. As smiles are meant to be shared, so is the good news of God's love and forgiveness. Let others know so they, too, can smile into the face of God.

SIMPLY SPEAKING

Every time you smile at someone, it is an action of love, a gift to that person, a beautiful thing.

MOTHER TERESA OF CALCUTTA

☺ LIVING THE GOD LIFE

Why not play the "smile game" today? See how many people you can get to smile at you—by smiling at them first. Not only is it a fun game, but everyone's a winner!

TREAT YOUR BODY LIKE A TEMPLE.

Don't you know that your body is the temple of the Holy Spirit,
who lives in you and was given to you by God?
You do not belong to yourself.

1 CORINTHIANS 6:19 NLT

The temple in Jerusalem was built for God following His precise instructions. Two bronze pillars at its entrance stood for "God establishes strength" (see 1 Kings 7:21). In the innermost section of this house of worship, the Most Holy Place was set apart. Within this Holy of Holies sat the Ark of the Covenant, the sacred chest that symbolized His presence. Inside the Ark were the stone tablets on which God wrote the Ten Commandments.

Only the best materials were used to construct and furnish God's temple. Everything and everyone in its service was purified and dedicated to the Lord.

Jesus referred to His own body as a temple. The apostle Paul told Christians their bodies were temples of the Holy Spirit. Do you look at your body in this way? If you belong to God, He dwells within your temple.

Once you recognize that your body is God's temple, your relationship with your body will change forever. You will want to care for it, making sure it is strong and healthy. You will be careful not to abuse it or pollute it, treating it respectfully and keeping it pure. And you will want to dedicate it to God's service.

Contemplate how to incorporate these ideals into your daily life. Discuss with God His plans for your temple and how you can use it to please Him. God will strengthen the pillars of your spiritual life.

Begin each morning with prayer and Bible reading to set the tone for the rest of the day. Hide God's Word within your heart by meditation and memorization. There, hidden within your most holy place, His Word symbolizes His presence.

As you treat your body like the temple it is, you will grow in your ability to live for God's glory. And His glory will fill your temple.

SIMPLY SPEAKING

The body is matter, but it is God's creation.
When it is neglected or scoffed at,
God himself is insulted.

MICHEL QUOIST

☺ LIVING THE GOD LIFE

*I*n what ways can you better care for your body,
the temple of the Holy Spirit?

GIVE HEED TO THE TEN COMMANDMENTS.

The LORD your God will delight in you if you obey his voice and keep
the commands and laws written in this Book of the Law, and if you
turn to the LORD your God with all your heart and soul.

DEUTERONOMY 30:10 NLT

Aren't the Ten Commandments just a bunch of ancient laws? No! Although given centuries ago, these basic rules for living are still applicable for modern times.

Rules and regulations are often considered in a negative light today, but in Hebrew (the original language of the Ten Commandments) the word *law* has a positive connotation. God gave His commands out of love and compassion for His people, to guide them as they sought to live rightly.

God's Top Ten detail how to relate to God and to others. The Lord demands exclusive worship because of who He is and what He has done. His refusal to share honor or affection with anyone else may sound dictatorial, but this command is actually for His children's protection. God knows the devastation that follows when people seek to serve other gods. In like manner, disobeying God's principles for human relations makes life miserable.

To help you better understand and heed God's commandments, study them in a modern paraphrase. Focus on the positive aspects of what you can do to follow each of these commands. For instance, you can go beyond the basics of honoring your parents by adding actions to your words. Find practical ways to help your father and mother, perhaps without their even knowing it.

Like the psalmist, you will discover great joy in reflecting on and practicing God's commands (see Psalm 119). Heeding God's Law is the most sensible way to live. Just as no one can change natural laws, such as the law of gravity, so it is impossible to alter the effect of God's spiritual laws—the Creator of the universe Himself sees to that.

SIMPLY SPEAKING

The Ten Commandments are not multiple choice.

AUTHOR UNKNOWN

☺ LIVING THE GOD LIFE

Why not take the time to memorize the Ten Commandments in a modern translation? You'll be hiding God's Word in your heart, and you'll be better able to focus on how to apply these commands to your daily life.

REMEMBER THAT GOD LOVES YOU.

The LORD has appeared of old to me, saying:
"Yes, I have loved you with an everlasting love;
Therefore with lovingkindness I have drawn you."

JEREMIAH 31:3 NKJV

God loves you! He really does! No matter what you've been led to believe. No matter what the circumstances of your life have been or what you may do in the future. God absolutely, undeniably, unconditionally loves you, and you couldn't get Him to stop loving you if you tried.

Until you know that—know it with certainty in your heart—you will not be able to move forward in your spiritual life. You will have no foundation of trust on which to build a close relationship with God.

The Bible says, "God is love" (1 John 4:8 NKJV). He is the eternal essence of love, and all love originates with Him. His deep, abiding love is far beyond the fading fancy of human affection. His love embodies acceptance, mercy, and sacrifice. You have no reason to fear God's love because, as the Bible says, perfect love drives away fear (see 1 John 4:18).

Abandon yourself to God's awesome love, and allow His love to make you complete in Him. You have nothing to lose but everything to gain by embracing the love God extends.

But be warned! Experiencing God's love will radically change your life. It will draw you into the most intimate relationship you have ever known. It seeks to replace self-centeredness with God-centeredness. It roots out the weeds threatening to overrun your spiritual garden and prunes and cultivates for maximum growth.

The love of God is never passive. His love calls you into service. Love cares, love gives, love helps, love listens. The torrent of God's love gushing through you will splash over onto others. You can't keep it to yourself. And you wouldn't want to.

SIMPLY SPEAKING

The person you are now, the person you have been, the person you will be—this person God has chosen as beloved.

WILLIAM COUNTRYMAN

☺ LIVING THE GOD LIFE

Why not spend some time today basking in God's presence, experiencing His love? Meditate on a favorite verse that focuses on God's love, such as John 3:16, and allow the Holy Spirit to make that love a reality in your heart.

THINK LIKE A CHILD.

[Jesus said,] I tell you as seriously as I know how that anyone who
refuses to come to God as a little child will never
be allowed into his Kingdom.

MARK 10:15 TLB

A child is naturally curious and asks question after question,
including the oft-repeated "Why?" Direct your curiosity toward
God. Learn more about Him. Don't be afraid to ask Him your
wildest questions.

A child seeks security and warm relationships. God offers
true security—eternal life—and desires a warm, intimate
relationship with you. Cultivate your relationship with God daily.

A child is eager and enthusiastic, full of the joy of life.
Rekindle your childlike enthusiasm and eagerly embrace the life
God has given you.

A child can find fun in most any situation. You can discover
great delight in living for God.

A child views things as totally right or totally wrong.
Adopting such a clear division between right and wrong can help
you quit wavering in the uncertain middle ground and decide to
choose right. God will direct you toward the proper path.

A child is honest and transparent, with no pretense or guile.

Drop any deceit. Choose to be open and sincere with people and with God. This may make you more vulnerable, but it also creates a deeper bond.

A child accepts truth and easily believes. God longs for you to believe His truth and let it make a difference in your life.

A child likes repetition. God never tires of your repeated petitions or declarations of "I love You." He also affirms His love for you over and over and over.

A child readily forgives and forgets. So does God. Why not try to do likewise?

Thinking like a child may appear to be simple, but it can bring profound results. Become as a little child, and draw closer to your heavenly Father.

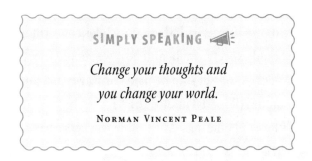

SIMPLY SPEAKING

Change your thoughts and
you change your world.

NORMAN VINCENT PEALE

☺ LIVING THE GOD LIFE

You are God's child, precious in His sight. How can you approach Him with a childlike attitude today?

PUT MONEY IN ITS PLACE.

*Those who love money will never have enough. How absurd to think
that wealth brings true happiness!*

ECCLESIASTES 5:10 NLT

The world says, "Money brings freedom," but desire for
wealth enslaves. Society advises, "Money offers security," but
riches quickly pass away. Culture claims, "Money provides power
and makes you successful," but true power and success come
only from God. The media sends the message "Money brings
happiness," yet that brand of happiness is short-lived.

So, what is the proper use of money? The Bible warns against
the love of currency, but you need it to live in today's world.
God's Word provides us with these principles concerning money,
what we should expect from it, and how we should use it:

- Wages. A worker is to be paid fair wages in a timely
  manner. (Read 1 Timothy 5:18.)
- Tithes and offerings. Most Bible teachers agree that 10
  percent of your income is the place to start. Additional
  money can be given as an offering to different causes as
  the Lord directs you. (Read 2 Corinthians 9:7.)
- Taxes. The Bible instructs us to pay our taxes, even if
  levied by an oppressive government. (Read Romans 13:7.)

- Debts. Debt is a form of slavery. Pay your debts promptly. The Bible urges us never to owe money to anyone. (Read Romans 13:8.)
- Usury. Don't charge exorbitant interest on loans. In fact, Moses instructed the Jews not to require any interest when loaning to a fellow Israelite. (Read Psalm 15:5.)
- Contentment. Be satisfied with what you have. True contentment is found only in the Lord. (Read Hebrews 13:5.)

Use money as a tool; don't allow it to run your life. Acknowledge God as the Source of all and the One to whom you must give account. Following His principles keeps money in its proper place.

SIMPLY SPEAKING

If a person gets his attitude toward money straight, it will help straighten out almost every other area in his life.

BILLY GRAHAM

☺ LIVING THE GOD LIFE

*H*ow can you use the money God has given you wisely and for His glory?

LIGHT THE LAMP OF GOD'S WORD INSIDE YOUR HEAD AND HEART.

Your word is a lamp to my feet and a light for my path.

PSALM 119:105

The Bible is for all intents and purposes a letter: a love letter, to be specific, documenting God's great love for mankind. He created us in His image, endowed us with a free will so that we would be free to return His love without coercion, and when we rebelled and rejected Him, He bought us back from the evil master to whom we had sold ourselves. This story of love given, love lost, and love redeemed is what the Bible is all about.

All letters have this ability to document and preserve important aspects of relationships between people. But of all letters, love letters are the most cherished. Often the recipients read them again and again, lingering at times on one portion and then on another. With time, the paper becomes worn and fragile—but that doesn't matter because the words have become etched on the heart and mind.

As you faithfully read the Bible—God's love letter to you—you may choose to meditate on one particular verse or passage and then another, soaking up the drama, the emotion, the wisdom and insight. Over time, those passages will become familiar. That's a good thing. Enhance the process by connecting key words with the reference (book, chapter, verse) in your mind. As you memorize God's Word, it becomes part of you. Embedded in the soil of your mind, it is able to spawn spiritual truth, which in turn gives birth to faith.

Don't neglect God's love letter to you. Read it often, meditate on it, pray over it, and entrust to memory at least one verse per week. It will soon get deep down inside you where it can do the most good.

SIMPLY SPEAKING 📢

The words of God which you receive by your ear,
hold fast in your heart. For the Word of God is
the food of the soul.

SAINT GREGORY I

☺ LIVING THE GOD LIFE

What verse will you memorize this week?

DEVELOP YOUR GIFTS AND TALENTS.

God gives [his people] many kinds of special abilities, but it is the same Holy Spirit who is the source of them all.

1 CORINTHIANS 12:4 TLB

The Lord has gifted each person with certain abilities, apportioning them as He sees fit. Whatever your talents, God expects you to use them to serve Him and others.

Do you wonder which gifts you have and how to use them? Here is a 3-D pattern to follow:

- Discover. Think about what you are good at and what you enjoy doing. What are your natural abilities? Pray and ask God to make these clear to you.

- Define. Ask others to help you determine your specific giftings and areas of service. Where and how do you feel called to minister using your gifts? You may also need to set some limits to avoid overwork and burnout.

- Develop. Practice your talent. Put it to work. Perfect it. Get training, if needed, to make your talent more productive and polished so you can achieve your potential and increase your effectiveness. This D can be a lifelong process. As you mature, continue to expand your ministry as the Lord leads.

Sometimes God will call you to serve in an area in which you feel you have no talent. When God calls, He also equips. He may want you to move away from your comfort zone to learn something new. Obey and step out in faith.

When such a call occurs, you can still follow the 3-D process, only with a bit of a twist. Discover what God wants you to do. Then define what you need to know and to be able to do to fulfill your new calling. Develop the skills needed to serve effectively.

As you grow in your own gifts, you will be better able to recognize the gifts of others. Use the knowledge and experience you've gained to assist others in their own talent discovery and development.

SIMPLY SPEAKING

No one can arrive from being talented alone.
God gives talent; work transforms talent
into genius.

ANNA PAVLOVA

☺ LIVING THE GOD LIFE

There are many spiritual gifts inventories available, through your local church, a Christian bookstore in your area, or online. These can give you an idea of the unique talents and abilities God has blessed you with, as well as suggestions of where to plug in to use those gifts for God's glory.

SEARCH FOR HIM WITH ALL YOUR HEART.

You will search again for the LORD your God. And if you search for him with all your heart and soul, you will find him.

DEUTERONOMY 4:29 NLT

Have you been searching for something to make you feel special? Are you looking for a friend? Seeking happiness? Do you long for love and peace? Did you think you had found what you wanted only to be disappointed and dissatisfied? That's because only God can fulfill your deep longings and needs. These suggestions will help you search for Him with all your heart:

- Look for God in His Word. Read it as if it were written especially for you with personal messages waiting to be disclosed—because it is.
- Listen for God when you pray. Quiet your mind and hear His whispers within.
- See God in other people. Whether or not they are Christians, God may reveal things to you through their lives. Discern what God is trying to show you through others.
- Find God in a worship service. Be open to connecting with Him at any and all times—during the music, the

reading of the Word, the pastor's message, a testimony, or even in giving an offering.

- Search for God in the hustle and bustle of life. He is in the midst of your hectic days.
- Seek God in the silence too. He often speaks with a still, small voice, and you need silence in order to tune into His frequency.

Your search for God should be ongoing. As you seek Him continually, you will get to know Him in new ways and keep growing closer until the day you meet face-to-face. There your search won't really end, for throughout eternity you can continue to explore all His amazing attributes.

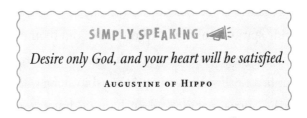

SIMPLY SPEAKING

Desire only God, and your heart will be satisfied.

AUGUSTINE OF HIPPO

☺ LIVING THE GOD LIFE

How has God spoken to you recently? Through His Word? Through a fellow believer? Through an answer to prayer? Thank Him for His faithfulness to draw near to you when you draw near to Him.

REPROGRAM YOUR RADIO.

Let the word of Christ dwell in you richly in all wisdom, teaching and admonishing one another in psalms and hymns and spiritual songs, singing with grace in your hearts to the Lord.

COLOSSIANS 3:16 NKJV

Have you ever heard the song "Turn Your Radio On"? It describes a radio station where the angels of heaven sing with the music. Maybe you don't experience such uplifting music when you listen to the radio. Consider tuning into a Christian radio station.

Rather than songs bemoaning sorrows or glorifying sin, seek ones offering spiritual solutions. Godly music can soothe and satisfy the soul, leaving the listener with a sense of peace and hope. Your heart will soar on wings of worship along with the music. As the language of the soul, such music draws your spirit to God and opens it to His truth.

Christian music goes beyond mere entertainment. Although its sounds do please the ear, this music fulfills higher purposes— to glorify God and to edify the listener. Its message should be clear and faithful to the Bible's teaching, communicating God's principles via a melody. When you hear truth set to a tune, you remember it.

Songs may speak about God or be addressed directly to Him in praise and prayer. Songs may share struggles and needs or recount God's blessings and express thanksgiving. Some talk about heaven, others about daily living. Christian music truly conveys the essence of the Christian life.

In the vast repertoire of Christian music, you will find something for a number of different tastes and moods. A fast-paced gospel song can chase away the doldrums as you drive to work. A reverent hymn might soothe your fussy infant as you rock her. Praise choruses could enliven your exercise time.

Become familiar with the vast library available on the airwaves. You're sure to find music to meet you right where you are and encourage you to grow closer to God. Christian music carries a living message, one that feeds the spirit.

SIMPLY SPEAKING
Praising God is one of the highest and purest acts of religion. In prayer we act like men; in praise we act like angels.
THOMAS WATSON

☺ LIVING THE GOD LIFE

What are your favorite radio stations? Easy listening? Country? Talk radio? Why not try a Christian radio station for a week and see what kind of difference it makes in your life?

RUN FROM THE GREEN-EYED MONSTER.

A heart at peace gives life to the body,
but envy rots the bones.

PROVERBS 14:30

Desiring to possess what belongs to someone else—whether it be good looks, a new car, a showcase home, or a spouse—is wrong. Such envy can consume you and lead to a life of dissatisfaction and sorrow.

In the Bible, the words translated as "envy" or "jealousy" come from the same original words in Hebrew (Old Testament) and Greek (New Testament). The meanings of these words in Scripture and their definitions in English reveal the negative aspects of these emotions.

Envy is a feeling of discontent and resentment over the possessions and achievements of another or the desire for what belongs to another. Jealousy means being suspicious and resentful of someone or hostile and envious of others' good fortune.

God's Word takes this idea even further, describing envy as rotten (see Prov. 14:30 NKJV) and a murderer (see Job 5:2), and jealousy as "cruel as the grave" (Song of Songs 8:6 NKJV). Envy can be found on God's list of sins that believers should get rid of because it leads to confusion and every evil.

The Lord takes envy seriously. In fact, He forbids it. God will deliver those being devoured by this green-eyed monster if they turn to Him for help. You cannot escape its clutches on your own.

Once you have been set free, you need to replace the negative feelings of jealousy and envy with positive ones. Leaving an empty space where they once thrived leaves you open to their return.

Allow God's love to flood your heart and life. His love brings with it peace and joy. It is kind and considerate. Such love never fails.

When envy rears its ugly head, flee to God and embrace His love. Only He can slay that monster.

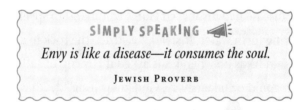

SIMPLY SPEAKING

Envy is like a disease—it consumes the soul.

JEWISH PROVERB

☺ LIVING THE GOD LIFE

What kinds of things are you most likely to envy in other people? Instead of focusing on what you don't have, why not focus on all of the blessings God has given you? When you do, you'll watch that green-eyed monster disappear.

LEARN TO TAKE "NO" FOR AN ANSWER.

Each time he said, "No. But I am with you; that is all you need. My
power shows up best in weak people." Now I am glad to boast about
how weak I am; I am glad to be a living demonstration of Christ's
power, instead of showing off my own power and abilities.

2 CORINTHIANS 12:9 TLB

No! At age two this may be a favorite word to repeat, but
most people do not like to be told no when they want to do
something.

God told Moses no. Moses could not enter the Promised
Land because he had disobeyed God's command to speak to the
rock to bring forth water. Instead, he struck the rock in anger.

God told Jesus no when Jesus asked if His cup of suffering
and death could be taken away. God knew Jesus' death was the
only way to pay for the sins of the world and provide eternal life.

God told Paul no. He would not remove Paul's thorn in the
flesh, but He would provide divine strength to overcome. His
strength is made perfect in weakness.

If God answers no to your request, He has something better
in mind for you. Yes may not be the best in this situation or
at this time. Perhaps saying yes to a mission trip would mean

adverse circumstances overseas, while the no that keeps you home opens the door for a campus ministry that results in many young people coming to know the Lord and growing in the faith.

No could be necessary for your health or safety or simply because what you are asking would interfere with God's best for you. You may never understand or know why. Trust God's wisdom. As parents refuse children candy before dinner or permission to play near danger, so God says no when it is for your good. Thank Him for the times He's said no in your life.

SIMPLY SPEAKING 📣

God has not always answered my prayers.
If he had, I would have married the wrong
man—several times!

RUTH BELL GRAHAM

☺ LIVING THE GOD LIFE

Has God given a resounding "No" in an answer to your prayers? Ultimately, it was because He had your best in mind. How did the situation turn out?

LET GO OF THE PAST.

No, dear brothers and sisters, I am still not all I should be, but I am
focusing all my energies on this one thing: Forgetting the past and
looking forward to what lies ahead.

PHILIPPIANS 3:13 NLT

If you want to grow closer to God, you must let go of the
past. The Bible says the past is good for only this: that we might
learn from our mistakes and remember the goodness of God.
When we belabor it, let it pull us down with guilt and shame or
disappointment and regret, it keeps us from being who we can
be in the present and from becoming who we are meant to be
in the future.

Living in the past can also mean falling back on past
triumphs and accomplishments. This too can be problematic.
Riding on the past can cause us to miss God's best and grow dull
and unproductive.

Lamentations 3:22–23 says, "The steadfast love of the
LORD never ceases, his mercies never come to an end; they are
new every morning" (NRSV). Each day with God is a new day,
a new beginning. Our past sins are forgiven and as such have
no negative or positive value. Great and small, they are of no
consequence. We are to abandon them on the road and walk

away with arms free to grasp the goodness of life stretching out before us.

Don't live your life in the past. Take hold of the days you have left, commit them to God, and walk forward into newness of life—fresh and pure. Ask God what purpose He has for you and tackle it with zeal. Be mindful that you are in His presence and that the future is still an unwritten book.

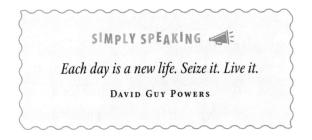

SIMPLY SPEAKING

Each day is a new life. Seize it. Live it.

DAVID GUY POWERS

☺ LIVING THE GOD LIFE

*D*etermine to put the past behind you and move on with life! How will you live for today, today?

FORGIVE YOURSELF.

"Come now, let us reason together," says the
Lord. "Though your sins are like scarlet,
they shall be as white as snow;
though they are red as crimson,
they shall be like wool."

ISAIAH 1:18

Forgiveness is essential to the Christian life. First of all,
acknowledgment of your sinful condition, along with repentance
and confession to God, results in His complete forgiveness and
your entry into fellowship with Him. Without forgiveness, you
would be lost.

When you slip and do wrong, confess your sin to God. He
will always forgive you, and He promises to remember it no
more. To experience God's cleansing forgiveness, however, you
must meet a condition. In order to be forgiven by God, Jesus
said, you must forgive others—including yourself (see Matt.
6:14). And that might be the most difficult thing of all.

You may not even know why it's difficult to forgive yourself
for past wrongs. It might be that your self-esteem is so low that
you just can't see yourself as happy, clean, and forgiven. You
might have the mistaken idea that there are some sins God can't

forgive, but Jesus' sacrifice on the cross was big enough to cover sin of all kinds. Maybe you look around and see the damage your sin has caused and feel you don't deserve to be forgiven. While we are to be sober and circumspect about the circumstances and hardships our sin has caused others, no good can come from continuing to punish ourselves and cutting ourselves off from God.

When we harbor unforgiveness in our hearts—even unforgiveness for ourselves—we distance ourselves from God. We decide that He was wrong to forgive us and we know better. Forget the posturing, the ego trips, and self-chastisement. Confess your sins to God, receive His miraculous pardon, and go on to live the life He created you to live.

SIMPLY SPEAKING

If God forgives us, we must forgive ourselves. Otherwise it is almost like setting up ourselves as a higher tribunal than him.

C. S. LEWIS

☺ LIVING THE GOD LIFE

For what do you need to forgive yourself today?

LEARN WHERE TO TURN IN TIMES OF TROUBLE.

God is our refuge and strength,
always ready to help in times of trouble.

PSALM 46:1 NLT

Just as a story must have conflict, so life will have troubles—that's simply a fact. No amount of complaining or wishing or manipulating will change this constant truth. You cannot talk it away, pray it away, or even live a good enough life to avoid it completely.

Sure, we do sometimes bring trouble on ourselves by making poor choices, repeating mistakes, ignoring wise counsel, or disobeying God's laws. But even if we were to walk perfectly, it would not be enough to hold back the tide of trouble and tribulations that surround us in this fallen world. The hope of Christianity is not that we will have no troubles but that God, in all His love and compassion, will come to our aid.

You may find this strange, but you can actually use trouble to grow closer to God. When it comes—and it will—run to Him and don't let Him out of your sight. Ask Him to bring His vast resources to bear on your behalf and to walk with you, hand in hand, until you can once again see a clear road before you.

God loves you and, like a good father, He's there for you whenever you need Him. Why would you want to face your problems alone when the almighty God of the universe is standing nearby, ready to help you? Bring your troubles to Him, lay them at His feet, and let Him help you sort it all out. You will not be turned away.

SIMPLY SPEAKING

The world can create trouble in peace, but God can create peace in trouble.

THOMAS WATSON

☺ LIVING THE GOD LIFE

What troubles are you facing right now? Why not place them in God's capable hands and allow Him to walk with you through the situation to the other side?

JUDGE NOT.

[Jesus said,] For in the same way you judge others, you will be judged, and with the measure you use, it will be measured to you.

MATTHEW 7:2

You have probably heard the remark, "Who made you my judge?" Perhaps this saying originally came from Jesus' teaching against harshly judging others.

When you sense the urge to criticize or condemn someone, mentally step back and reassess the situation. Avoid stereotyping others or jumping to conclusions. You simply can't know what is in another person's heart.

At first glance, it would seem that this instruction was given for the benefit of the one being judged, and certainly it was. But it was also given for the benefit of the person who is doing the judging. Are you aware that judging others can actually be more damaging to you than it is to them?

Judgment can be passed down only by one who is himself flawless and irreproachable. If the one who judges has also sinned, he will bring down judgment on his own head. Only God is perfect. Only God is qualified to judge others.

If you wish to grow closer to God, you must be willing to acknowledge that He alone is the great Judge of all mankind.

He alone is able to see the hearts of men and women and deal with them accordingly. You must be willing to stand before Him yourself robed in grace and a contrite heart.

When you are tempted to judge, simply pass that upward to a higher authority. Turn a deaf ear to the voice that would say it is your responsibility to set someone else straight. That's a trick of the devil that will lead you into dangerous territory. Submit instead to your Father's instruction to leave it at His feet.

SIMPLY SPEAKING

The more you judge, the less you love.

HONORE DE BALZAC

☺ LIVING THE GOD LIFE

Think of one person whom you frequently find yourself judging. Does this person have any positive attributes? Why not share your positive thoughts with that person? You just might make his or her day!

PRAY, PRAY, PRAY.

Pray all the time.

1 THESSALONIANS 5:17 MSG

Jesus told a story about two men in church who prayed.
One, a leader in his congregation, stood near the front of the
sanctuary. He did not kneel humbly but stood. He made excuses
by comparing himself to the other man: "I'm glad I'm not like
him." The other man stood in the back, and couldn't even bring
himself to lift his head, as if he couldn't bear to look at God. He
was ashamed of what he'd done—and who he was. He couldn't
do anything but pound on his chest and say, "God, forgive me;
I'm a sinner." (Read Luke 18:9–14.)

Those looking on might have imagined the first man being
the one closest to God, but through His story Jesus was saying
that just the opposite is true. The second man, the one who was
honest with God concerning the true condition of his heart, was
the one who grew closer to God.

You can grow closer to God only when your prayers are
truthful, humble, and contrite. God isn't impressed with fancy
words and proud prayers. He wants you to open your heart to
Him—honestly and sincerely. It's then that He can come in and
do His work. It's then that He can make you a person who is

comfortable in His presence. Just speak to Him often throughout your day. Tell Him how you really feel—He knows anyway—and you will soon feel closer to God than you ever imagined you could be.

SIMPLY SPEAKING

*Only that prayer which comes from God's heart
can get to God's heart.*

C. H. SPURGEON

☺ LIVING THE GOD LIFE

Why not take a new approach to prayer? Instead of praying
in your usual place, take a prayer walk. Not only will you enjoy
God's beautiful creation, but you will also experience a new
vitality in your quiet time with Him.

FIND A CHURCH.

*Let us not neglect our church meetings, as some people do, but
encourage and warn each other, especially now that the day of his
coming back again is drawing near.*

HEBREWS 10:25 TLB

Local religious congregations have played a vital role in
community life since Bible times. Paul and the apostles preached
in synagogues and churches as they spread the gospel. The local
assembly functioned as the heart of the religious community.

Although much has changed since the first century,
Christians still need connection with a local body of believers.
A healthy church has much to offer for developing dynamic
spiritual lives.

A good church provides: (1) A place for instruction—
teaching the Bible and how to live it out in daily life; (2) a place
for prayer, where people can share requests and be supported
by others who pray with and for them; (3) an opportunity for
fellowship at worship services and social events; (4) a place to
observe the Lord's Supper in Communion, as Christ said to do in
remembrance of Him.

The church exists to: share God's good news, help those in
need, send and support missionaries, and encourage members to

serve as God has called and equipped them. Churches reach out in many ways: soup kitchens, food pantries, Christian schools, child care, youth activities, support groups, etc. Church is a place to give and to receive, to be a blessing and to be blessed.

What should you look for in a church? Seek one that honors Jesus Christ and His Word, one that preaches Bible truths, not just man's ideas. One with meaningful worship. One that expresses warmth and affirmation—one that is friendly, kind, and hospitable. Search for one that serves the community and also has outreach through missions. Find one that uses the gifts and abilities of everyone, not just a select few.

Be willing to become an active participant. You need the church, and the church needs you.

SIMPLY SPEAKING 📣

Church-goers are like coals in a fire. When they cling together, they keep the flame aglow; when they separate, they die out.

BILLY GRAHAM

☺ LIVING THE GOD LIFE

Are you currently involved in a church family of your own? If not, make the commitment to begin looking for a body of believers in which you can participate.

MEDITATE ON GOD'S WORD.

They delight in doing everything God wants them to, and day and night are always meditating on his laws and thinking about ways to follow him more closely.

PSALM 1:2 TLB

Meditation has gotten a bad rap in the last twenty years, conjuring up images of people sitting in yoga positions and humming to align themselves with the universe. It's too bad, because meditation, which simply means "to reflect," is a beneficial tool for Christians and is mentioned many times in the Bible.

When Joshua took over leadership of the Israelites after Moses' death, God told him to meditate on His Law day and night so he would be careful to observe it (see Josh. 1:8). Israel's kings were also instructed to read and meditate on God's Word each day. The Psalms speak of meditating in your heart all day long and through the night.

Reflecting on God's precepts, His principles, His works, and His ways enlightens the mind, uplifts the spirit, and provides wisdom. Pondering God's Word and mentally exploring its depths of meaning and application helps in putting it into practice in your life. Memorizing Scripture allows you to carry God's Word with you so you can draw on it anywhere, anytime.

Spiritual meditation often evokes praise. Sometimes it inspires a song, a poem, or other creative work. The practice of meditation will help prepare you for Bible study, worship, music, artistic endeavor, or just daily life.

Take time to contemplate God, His characteristics, His names, and His truth. Consider His holiness. Think about your relationship with Him. With endless possibilities to imagine, meditating on God and His Word will never grow dull. Each time seems fresh and new because God's Word is alive and powerful. Don't miss out on such a wonderful experience. Meditation will bless both you and God.

SIMPLY SPEAKING 📢

When you meditate, imagine that Jesus Christ in person is about to talk to you about the most important thing in the world. Give him your complete attention.

G. FÉNELON

☺ LIVING THE GOD LIFE

If you're not used to meditating, try this: take a favorite passage and begin to read it. As you read it, think about what each verse is saying and write it down. If a word jumps out at you, look it up in a dictionary and meditate on the meaning. How does it apply to you?

MAKE HIM LORD OF YOUR LIFE.

If you confess with your mouth, "Jesus is Lord," and believe in your heart that God raised him from the dead, you will be saved.

ROMANS 10:9

Getting to know God better means more than just learning about Him. It means cultivating a close personal relationship with Him—relating person to person, one-on-one. As you become better acquainted with God, you become more aware of His awesomeness. God is all-powerful, all-knowing, infinite, and completely holy.

The Bible states that there is one God and one Lord, Jesus Christ, who made all things, and all authority has been given unto Him. Jesus is not simply one among many, but the only path to heaven. He said, "I am the way and the truth and the life. No one comes to the Father except through me" (John 14:6). While on earth, Jesus claimed to be Lord and accepted recognition as Lord from His followers. When you call Jesus "Lord," you acknowledge His preeminence.

When you accept Jesus Christ as your personal Savior, you should also acknowledge Him as your Lord. Making Jesus Lord of your life means surrendering everything to Him and yielding to His authority. Is there any area of your life you are trying to

keep under your own control? Give it up to the Lord. Ask God
to help you submit to Him. In the process, you will receive more
than you give from His hand.

Seek always to put Christ first. Make a conscious effort to
live for Him, not for yourself. Living in subjection to the Lord
may sound limiting, but it is actually liberating. It frees you from
bondage to selfishness and fills you with His inexpressible joy.

Whether people yield to Jesus as Lord or not, He still holds
that position over the universe. Someday every knee will bow
and every tongue confess that Jesus Christ is Lord. You have the
opportunity to recognize Jesus as your Lord right now. Why wait?

SIMPLY SPEAKING

*Christ is either both Savior and Lord, or he is
neither Savior nor Lord.*

JOHN R. DEWITT

☺ LIVING THE GOD LIFE

Is there any area of your life that you need to surrender to the
lordship of Christ? Write a prayer to Him, giving Him complete
control and submitting to His will in all things. Your life will be
happier and more peaceful as a result.

COUNT YOUR BLESSINGS.

How we praise God, the Father of our Lord Jesus Christ, who has blessed us with every spiritual blessing in the heavenly realms because we belong to Christ.

EPHESIANS 1:3 NLT

Thousands suffered devastating losses from the terrible tsunami of December 2004 and from Hurricane Katrina. Such catastrophes often cause people to pause and consider all they have to be thankful for. It is easy to take blessings for granted. Whether you feel prosperous or overwhelmed with needs, counting your blessings will encourage you and strengthen your appreciation for what you do have.

Anytime and anyplace are appropriate for taking stock of your blessings. You may simply keep a mental record, or you might wish to write them down and continue to add to the list as you think of them. The wonderful thing is that as you count them, your blessings seem to multiply. One leads to another, then to another. After all, the original meaning of the word *blessing* conveys the idea of abundance.

Begin with yourself—your talents, knowledge, experiences, reputation, health, and life itself. Make your list specific and personal. Next, move on to your family and home, friends, vocation, community, nation, and so on. Continue to expand your view. Include the intangible too: love, joy, peace, comfort, freedom, beauty, etc. Record things you enjoy and appreciate, such as nature, art, and music. What about technology?

Of course, you will want to include spiritual blessings, like God's Word and eternal life. The most important and lasting blessings in the Christian's life are spiritual in nature.

Where do all these blessings come from? Ultimately, from God, the Source of all good things. He is the All-Sufficient One who promised to supply all your needs and to give you abundant life. So don't just count all your blessings, thank God for them too.

SIMPLY SPEAKING

Reflect upon your present blessings, of which every man has many, not on your past misfortunes, of which all men have some.

CHARLES DICKENS

☺ LIVING THE GOD LIFE

Take stock of your blessings! Make a list of all the things God has done for you—and then thank Him for them!

CONTEMPLATE ETERNITY.

God has made everything beautiful for its own time. He has planted eternity in the human heart, but even so, people cannot see the whole scope of God's work from beginning to end.

ECCLESIASTES 3:11 NLT

Do you spend much time thinking about the future? Planning and preparing are common activities. But such provisions usually focus on life here on earth. What about the hereafter? Your brief life here is a mere speck in the expanse of eternity.

Someday every person will face an eternal destiny. For those who belong to the Lord Jesus Christ, a wonderful eternity awaits. Life everlasting with the Savior will exceed the bounds of human imagination. Scripture provides glimpses into that timeless future to help you anticipate its wonders.

God created time when He formed the world. Although you exist in this dimension now, you were made for eternity. One aspect of being created in God's image is immortality—not for the body but for the soul. A natural curiosity about eternity and desire to understand the meaning of life characterize this facet of human nature, which longs to explore the unknown. The Hebrew word translated "everlasting" in the Bible carries the meaning of "hidden" or "unknown time."

In that forever future there will be no more sickness, pain, sadness, or death. The curse from sin will be gone, and there will no longer be any darkness or night. Jesus said He was returning to heaven to prepare places for His followers, who will be His joint-heirs and reign with Him forever. They will receive rewards and eternal glory for their service to Him. They will walk streets of gold in their glorious resurrection bodies and feast at the marriage banquet of the Lord. They will see the new heaven and the new earth and the new Jerusalem.

God has prepared eternity for you and you for eternity. Pondering such magnificent infinity prompts praise to the Lord. Contemplating eternity gives you a head start on experiencing its joys—and they will never end.

SIMPLY SPEAKING

I thank thee, O Lord, that thou hast so set eternity within my heart that no earthly thing can ever satisfy me wholly.

JOHN BAILLIE

☺ LIVING THE GOD LIFE

Why not spend some time thanking God for the amazing future that awaits you in heaven?

LISTEN . . . AND KEEP LISTENING.

*Dear brothers and sisters, be quick to listen, slow to speak,
and slow to get angry.*

JAMES 1:19 NLT

To hear—really hear—what someone is saying, you must
stop and listen. You must focus your attention, open your mind
and heart, and avoid distractions. The same is true when you
want to hear what God is saying. To hear Him, you must listen
for Him, seek His person, and listen to Him. Learn to recognize
His voice. God speaks so you can understand. His words are not
a foreign language. He desires to communicate with you.

How does God speak? Throughout history He has spoken
in various ways: through prophets, angels, visions, dreams,
ordinary people, circumstances, the conscience, aloud, and
through the Bible.

Today God usually speaks directly to the heart. It may be
a thought or an impression or a verse that jumps out at you
when you read Scripture. Listen with your internal ear. Don't
be selective in your hearing. Make sure you hear the Lord and
not just your own thoughts. His speech always lines up with His
written Word.

Pay close attention to God's still, small voice. Place His

message above anything other people tell you. Listening to God will lead to wisdom. Obeying what He says will keep you from going astray. Heeding God's voice will result in spiritual growth and draw you closer to Him.

Your prayer time should not be all talking or asking. Much of this time should be devoted to listening to the Lord. Wait on Him. He will speak. He will reveal His character and His will for your life. If the message does not seem clear, tell Him, and ask for clarity. He does not want you to be confused.

Expect God to talk to you. Then listen carefully.

SIMPLY SPEAKING

Lord, teach me to silence my own heart
that I may listen to the gentle movement of the
Holy Spirit within me and sense the depths
which are of God.

ELIJAH DE VIDAS

☺ LIVING THE GOD LIFE

How has God spoken to you recently? What did He say? More importantly, how did you respond?

MEET WITH HIM FIRST THING EVERY MORNING.

*Each morning I will look to you in heaven and lay my requests before
you, praying earnestly.*

PSALM 5:3 TLB

The Bible records many instances where people got up early
to spend time with God. Even Jesus practiced this discipline.
Starting your day with the Lord establishes the tone for the rest
of the day. By setting aside time for God first thing each morning,
you illustrate the number-one priority He has in your life.

Greet God when you awaken, even before getting out of bed.
You can praise Him for a new day and thank Him for bringing
you safely through the night.

Spend time communing with the Lord before becoming
caught up in the hectic schedule of daily life. Even if you have
only a brief period, pray and read the Bible. This spiritual
nourishment will strengthen you for the day ahead and help you
be prepared for whatever comes.

Choose a Scripture or a word from the Lord gleaned
during your morning devotions. Meditate on this throughout
the day. You may want to write it on a note card to carry
with you or to post where you will see it often.

Meeting with God could also include singing or reading the words to a hymn. Worship God for who He is, and praise Him for what He has done. Pray for others and for yourself. Seek God's guidance and blessing for your daily activities. Thank Him for answers to prayer. Talk with Him as you would with a friend.

Your morning appointment with God will become so dear to you that it will become a habit you never want to break. As you bless God each morning and dedicate your day to Him, He pours blessings on you. This divine engagement is one you won't want to miss.

SIMPLY SPEAKING

Let your first "Good morning" be to
your Father in heaven.

KARL G. MAESER

☺ LIVING THE GOD LIFE

*W*hy not set your alarm an hour earlier and spend that time with God, reading His Word, meditating on His blessings, and getting His take on your upcoming day?

ATTEND A CHRISTIAN RETREAT.

Jesus said, "Come to me, all of you who are weary and carry heavy burdens, and I will give you rest."

MATTHEW 11:28 NLT

Life on this whirling planet sometimes seems as if it is spinning out of control. You get so caught up in the day-to-day survival mode you feel you can hardly catch your breath.

When your world becomes too intense and chaotic, or before it even reaches that state, pull away for a time of refreshment and renewal. A Christian retreat could be just what you need for rest and restoration—physically, mentally, emotionally, and spiritually.

In military terms, a retreat means moving back or withdrawing from the conflict to a place of safety. During His busy ministry on earth, Jesus pulled away and sought refreshment with the Father. He also called His disciples to come apart from the crowds and rest. A spiritual retreat provides a respite away from the demands and drudgery of daily life.

Many Christian organizations and retreat centers have programs designed to meet a variety of needs. Some retreats are silent, where you spend much time one-on-one with the Lord, allowing Him to minister to you personally. Most retreats are filled with spiritual teaching, similar to a seminar. They may also include times of recreation or organized activities.

The purpose of a Christian retreat is to help participants focus on God, listen to Him, and learn from Him. Jesus desires to set people free from their burdens. He offers healing and deliverance. A retreat can be an ideal setting to receive such blessings from the Lord. It might even be a life-changing experience.

The pause a Christian retreat offers allows time to reflect on your past and to prepare for the future. From this period of refreshment and renewal you will gain new strength to face whatever may come.

SIMPLY SPEAKING

Take rest; a field that has rested
gives a bountiful crop.

OVID

☺ LIVING THE GOD LIFE

$\mathcal{L}$ook into upcoming Christian retreats taking place in your area. The benefits of attending will far outweigh the cost!

TURN OFF THE TELEVISION.

Summing it all up, friends, I'd say you'll do best by filling your minds and meditating on things true, noble, reputable, authentic, compelling, gracious—the best, not the worst; the beautiful, not the ugly; things to praise, not things to curse.

PHILIPPIANS 4:8 MSG

Television may provide information, education, and entertainment, but it also offers much that detracts and distracts from a godly lifestyle. Unfortunately, many people appear unable to find a balance between using television as an educational tool and a mode of entertainment and totally drowning themselves in the avalanche of programming and marketing.

Give your eyes, ears, and mind a rest. At first, the stillness may be a shock to your system—but don't rush to fill it with other noise. Accept the quietness and savor it.

Cultivate times of silence. Don't fear them. Use them for your benefit. Take advantage of the quiet to listen to the Lord. Allow His presence to permeate your life. Talk with Him in your mind or out loud. Let God bring clarity to your thinking and to your living.

If you are used to the television blaring away every day, try turning it off one evening or one hour at first. Besides using this free time for quiet reflection, you could read a good book, visit or play a game with your family, do a craft, take a walk, or any number of activities. You may enjoy these alternatives so much you will want to increase your free-from-TV time. Could you give it up for a week? A month? Completely? You decide.

Growing closer to God takes time, and television is a time hog. Learn to moderate your use of it and you will find your life wonderfully free to pursue what really matters. You'll find that time you've been missing to get to know the One who will change your life forever.

SIMPLY SPEAKING

I find television very educational. Every time someone switches it on, I go into another room and read a good book.

GROUCHO MARX

☺ LIVING THE GOD LIFE

Try turning off the television for one evening this week. What interesting or exciting activities could you do instead?

SHARE YOUR FAITH.

In your hearts set apart Christ as Lord. Always be prepared to give an answer to everyone who asks you to give the reason for the hope that you have. But do this with gentleness and respect.

1 PETER 3:15

Before Jesus returned to heaven after His resurrection, He told His followers to go and make disciples of all nations. Still today, believers continue to carry out this great commission.

The terms *evangelism* and *witnessing* may sound overwhelming, but sharing your faith does not have to be intimidating. When you know some exciting news, aren't you eager to share it?

Sharing your faith can be as simple as telling others what Jesus has done for you, the difference He has made in your life. This message is too marvelous to keep all to yourself. Your joy and enthusiasm should compel you to speak up.

Whom can you tell? Everyone—your family, friends, neighbors, coworkers, acquaintances, salesmen, anyone you meet. You can steer conversations to spiritual topics and bring in your own faith experience. You might create curiosity by asking questions like, "Would you like to go to a place where you'll never get sick?" or "Can I tell you about my best friend, Jesus?"

When possible, build relationships with trust to gain the right to be heard. If others respect you, they will usually listen to what you have to say. But don't pass up those onetime opportunities. When God opens the door, go through it. If people are not very receptive, don't be discouraged. Even Jesus was not well received by everyone. Pray for God to continue to speak to them.

In fact, prayer should be part of your action plan. Pray before, during, and after sharing your faith. The Holy Spirit will prepare hearts and give you the right words to say. There is no pat formula.

Remember, too, that your actions often speak louder than your words. Make sure your life is a fitting testimony of God's goodness and love for others to see.

SIMPLY SPEAKING

We are the Bibles the world is reading; we are the creeds the world is needing; we are the sermons the world is heeding.

BILLY GRAHAM

LIVING THE GOD LIFE

When was the last time you shared the love of Jesus with someone else?

COOPERATE WITH THE WORK OF THE HOLY SPIRIT.

God has actually given us his Spirit (not the world's spirit) so we can know the wonderful things God has freely given us.

1 CORINTHIANS 2:12 NLT

The Holy Spirit takes an active role in the lives of believers. He indwells all who belong to God and bears witness that they are His. He equips each for whatever tasks He assigns.

A saying goes, "You have all of the Holy Spirit, but does He have all of you?" For the Holy Spirit to work most effectively in and through you, you must completely yield to Him. Don't try to run things yourself or hold back anything from His total control.

Imagine! You have God's Spirit living inside you—the almighty God who rules the universe. As Paul said, "Your body is a temple of the Holy Spirit" (1 Cor. 6:19). He is as much God as Jesus and the Father are—three persons in one God—and that's why the Holy Spirit knows and understands the deep things of God the Father. He will reveal them to believers who accept these truths.

Don't resist the Spirit, but cooperate with Him. He wants to abundantly bless your life. He will lead and guide. He will anoint you for His service. He will bring to mind the truths of Scripture.

He will teach you and impart godly wisdom. He will give comfort and courage and help you in every situation. He will correct when you err. He will empower you to resist temptation and restrain you from sin. He will increase your faith. He will bring healing. He is always with you—the guarantee of your eternal inheritance.

All this and more the Holy Spirit does for those who let Him have His way in their lives. He also freely gives the fruit of the Spirit and spiritual gifts to believers. All God's gifts are good, especially the gift of His Holy Spirit. Let Him transform your life.

SIMPLY SPEAKING

What other help could we ever need than that of the Holy Spirit of God?

ANDREA GARNEY

☺ LIVING THE GOD LIFE

Why not cooperate with the Holy Spirit today? Thank Him for the guidance, comfort, and wisdom He brings.

JOIN A BIBLE STUDY GROUP.

All Scripture is God-breathed and is useful for teaching, rebuking,
correcting and training in righteousness, so that the man of God may
be thoroughly equipped for every good work.

2 TIMOTHY 3:16–17

In the apostle Paul's second letter to Timothy, he wrote, "Study and be eager and do your utmost to present yourself to God approved (tested by trial), a workman who has no cause to be ashamed, correctly analyzing and accurately dividing [rightly handling and skillfully teaching] the Word of Truth" (2 Tim. 2:15 AMP).

God desires us to be well acquainted with His Word and know how to accurately share it with others. What better way to do this than to become a part of a local Bible study group? Most churches have many study groups to choose from. Some utilize different books of the Bible; some study different topics like marriage or raising godly children.

Whatever group you select, you are sure to discover new things you did not know about the Bible as well as develop relationships with other believers. And both of these will strengthen you in your own walk with the Lord.

God's Word breathes life into our impoverished souls.

Through it we learn more about God. It convicts us of sin. It points the way we should go. It helps us to live as reflections of Christ. It empowers us to be Christ to everyone around us.

When we study God's Word with other believers, we gain insight from people who have made the same mistakes that we do. Through the give-and-take of a Bible study group, we encourage one another to think and respond as Jesus would.

You, too, can be strengthened by studying God's Word with other believers.

SIMPLY SPEAKING

Studying the Bible with other Christians, sharing insights, reinforcing proper context is an essential complement to personal study.

ANDREA GARNEY

☺ LIVING THE GOD LIFE

Are you currently in a Bible study group with other believers? If not, check with your local church to find one that's right for you. Your walk with God will become more meaningful and vibrant as you grow together with other Christians.

WALK IN LOVE.

We love because he first loved us.

1 JOHN 4:19

The leader of a mission to the homeless was once asked why he would spend forty years of his life working with grimy, drunken, homeless people. His reply? "All I'm doing is giving back to others a little of the love God has shown to me."

Earlier in his life, the man had also been homeless. One day he stumbled into a shelter for a bowl of chili but experienced a taste of something much better: the love of Christ. A man that day told him that Jesus loved him despite his sin and shame. Convicted, the homeless man gave his life to Jesus and became a new person.

Out of gratitude for being saved, the man returned to the mission to share the love of Jesus with others. Was it difficult for him to reach out to other homeless people? Of course not, because he remembered where he had once been.

Really, that story belongs to all of us. On our own, we're all homeless, desperate, pitiful. We don't find Jesus, Jesus finds us. Even the love we give to others doesn't begin with us, it begins with Jesus demonstrating His love for us by dying on a cross for our sins.

The love we share, then, is really based in gratitude. We walk in love toward others to the extent that we remember God's love for us. Interestingly enough, when we love others with a heart of gratitude, we discover that we're really loving God back. One of the best ways to love God and grow closer to Him is to simply love those around us.

Take a moment to think of someone who needs the kind of love you have received from God. Now love that person—and know that through that person you are also loving God.

SIMPLY SPEAKING

God loved the world. Go thou and do likewise.

ERWIN W. LUTZER

☺ LIVING THE GOD LIFE

*W*ho needs to receive your love today?

SIT STILL FOR A SUNSET.

The Mighty One, God, the LORD, *speaks and summons the earth*
from the rising of the sun to the place where it sets.

PSALM 50:1

Have you ever taken an evening walk only to be stopped by
the beauty of a sunset?

Hues of purple, blue, gray, and orange streaking across the
western sky seem to strike a sense of awe in us no matter what
we're doing. Why do sunsets affect us the way they do?

Sunsets remind us that beauty exists beyond our control.
Beauty happens and to a great extent, it has nothing to do with
us. We can paint beautiful portraits of mountainous landscapes
and breathtaking vistas, but we can't match the daily portrait
God paints 365 days a year. And equally amazing: every day the
portrait is different.

But you can't have a painting without a painter. On a deeper
level, the sunset reminds us of God. He takes the time to paint
the sunset, then turns the painting around and shares it with us.
No one forces Him to share His masterpieces; He does it because
He wants us to enjoy them as He does. And He wants us to enjoy
Him.

So really, sunsets are an opportunity for worship. They

inspire us to break out in words of worship and praise to God. The next time you're taking an evening walk and you see a portrait unfolding before your eyes, don't keep walking. Stop. Stand still for a moment and enjoy it. Clap your hands in applause for the Painter. Compliment God on His handiwork and tell Him how great He is.

God doesn't need to be reminded of His greatness, but we do. We need sunsets to remember how small we are and how big He is. And we need to be reminded that the Painter is sharing a sunset with us simply because He wants us to enjoy Him too.

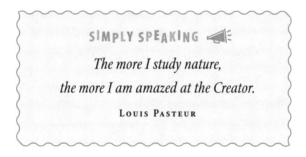

SIMPLY SPEAKING

The more I study nature,
the more I am amazed at the Creator.

LOUIS PASTEUR

☺ LIVING THE GOD LIFE

Why not take the time to watch the sunset this evening and remind the Creator of His greatness and goodness to you?

REPLACE NEGATIVE THOUGHTS WITH GOD'S PROMISES.

Do not conform any longer to the pattern of this world, but be transformed by the renewing of your mind.

ROMANS 12:2

When you turn on a computer, have you noticed that it usually follows the same routine? A short melody tells you that everything is going according to plan. Then the "wallpaper" appears, establishing your screen's backdrop. Next, icons dot the wallpaper followed by any applications your computer may have been programmed to open. Of course, this happens until something goes wrong.

The computer's routine is simply obeying a set of commands called its default settings. All things being equal, computers follow the instructions programmed on their hard drives.

And we're no different. We all have default settings—behaviors that just come naturally. All things being equal, we react the same way in given situations. The Bible gives it a name: flesh. Our flesh is the part of us that craves sin and darkness and anything else that draws us away from God.

One fleshly default setting common to everyone is negativity. Negativity is the attitude that this life is all there is. Situations won't change. People can't change. We're unable to change.

But from the Bible's perspective, we no longer need to regard people from a worldly point of view. Our perspective isn't based on this world; it's based on the love of our heavenly Father. The Bible is full of His promises. And what are they? That He loves us. He lives in us. Our value comes from him. Situations and people can change—including you! There's another word for this—hope—and it works in the opposite direction of negativity and draws us to God.

So exchange your negative thoughts for promises and you'll find yourself focusing on the One who makes the promises: God.

SIMPLY SPEAKING

Think positively and masterfully, with confidence and faith, and life becomes more secure, more fraught with action, richer in achievement and experience.

EDDIE RICKENBACKER

☺ **LIVING THE GOD LIFE**

Why not make a list of as many of God's promises as you can? Keep that list handy—perhaps on your bathroom mirror or refrigerator. When negative thoughts come, immediately remind yourself of the promises of God—and of the faithful One who made those promises.

FIND A PRAYER PARTNER.

[Jesus said,] Where two or three come together in my name,
there am I with them.

MATTHEW 18:20

Every year, countless hikers die from exposure or injury. Most troubling is the fact that many hiking fatalities could have been prevented. Someone chose to hike alone, encountered a problem, and was unable to receive the help even one person could have provided.

A cardinal rule in mountain climbing is that every hiker must have a partner. If a storm suddenly appears, an avalanche rumbles down the mountain, or the hiker falls and gets hurt, someone is there to assist.

Prayer is like mountain climbing. Sometimes the hike is easy, like a downhill walk. But other times, it's nothing short of an uphill climb: strenuous, overwhelming, exhausting. And if you fall and hurt yourself when no one is around, who will be there to help you?

Jesus told His followers not only to pray by themselves, but to find at least one other person to pray with them. In fact, Jesus promises to be present in a special way when at least two people join together in prayer.

If you don't already have one, find a prayer partner who will pray with you on a regular basis. Ask someone who makes you feel comfortable, someone who will encourage you along the terrain of mountains and valleys that compose your everyday walk with Jesus.

When you meet with your prayer partner, don't worry about acting spiritual or praying profound prayers. Just be yourself with your partner and with God. Share your joys, frustrations, and sorrows. Pray for your needs and your partner's. And don't forget to thank God for blessing you in so many ways—which includes giving you a prayer partner.

SIMPLY SPEAKING

As it is the business of tailors to make clothes and of cobblers to mend shoes, so it is the business of Christians to pray.

MARTIN LUTHER

☺ LIVING THE GOD LIFE

Do you have a prayer partner? If not, whom could you ask to pray with you on a regular basis?

BE FAITHFUL.

His master said to him, "Well done, good and faithful servant.
You have been faithful over a little; I will set you over much.
Enter into the joy of your master."

MATTHEW 25:21 ESV

If you were to study the stories of the great men and women
in the Bible, you would quickly see that their lives were filled
with hardship and adversity. These are just a few examples:

- Sarah, Abraham's wife, spent most of her adult life
  grieving her inability to have children.
- David, Israel's greatest king, survived an insurrection led
  by his own son Absalom.
- Mary, the mother of Jesus, experienced scathing criticism
  because she was an unwed mother.
- And, of course, Jesus was wrongly accused, ridiculed,
  betrayed, beaten, slandered, and nailed to a cross.

The common thread the great men and women of the Bible
shared is faithfulness. Despite the sorrow, pain, or mockery they
faced, they continued believing God was powerful, good, and
trustworthy. Some may have faltered, like Peter who denied Jesus
three times, but in the end, they remained faithful.

Faithfulness isn't an easy job. In fact, faithfulness is an

impossible job. *What?* you may say to yourself. *I can be faithful!*
But let's be honest. Can anyone be faithful without someone
from the outside supplying strength and encouragement to
continue in the face of difficulty? And who gives us that strength
and encouragement? Ultimately, it comes from God. That's why
the Bible tells us that faithfulness is a fruit of the Spirit, the fruit
of the Holy Spirit's work in us.

Being faithful means being full of faith—faith that God is
powerful, good, and trustworthy. When you encounter pain
and sorrow, don't focus on it. Focus on the God who gives you
strength and encouragement. Through this you'll discover that
God is bigger than any problem and able to sustain you, regardless of how overwhelming your situation might seem. And as a
result, you'll find that God is enabling you to be faithful.

SIMPLY SPEAKING ◀

*I long to accomplish a great and noble task, but
it is my chief duty to accomplish small tasks as if
they were great and noble.*

HELEN KELLER

☺ LIVING THE GOD LIFE

How have you been faithful in the difficulties you have faced?
How can you continue to be faithful in the future?

JUST SKIP IT!

*Is not this the fast that I choose: to loose the bonds of injustice,
to undo the thongs of the yoke, to let the oppressed go free,
and to break every yoke?*

ISAIAH 58:6 NRSV

We all know a little bit about fasting. We know that it means sacrifice, giving up a meal or some other perceived necessity in order to spend time with God, learning His ways and following His purpose.

These are the most common types of fasts engaged in today:

1. The Normal Fast. Abstaining from all solid and liquid food except for water.

2. The Absolute Fast. Abstaining from both food and drink.

3. The Partial Fast. Abstaining from particular foods, such as beef and chicken.

4. The Daniel Fast. Abstaining from everything except fruits, vegetables, and water.

5. The Juice Fast. Abstaining from everything except fruit and vegetable juices.

The duration of your fast and the type of fast you choose are completely up to you. But even the shortest fast, coupled with fervent prayer, can have amazing results because it takes our eyes off the things of the world and focuses our attention on God. Note: Do not fast without first getting your doctor's permission.

If you have a hurdle to jump in your life—an addiction, recurring sin, health issue, or an inability to hear God clearly concerning a particular decision—try fasting along with your prayer. Ask God to help you see what you could not see before. Ask Him to give you wisdom and counsel concerning the issue.

It's also a good strategy to keep a notebook and pen nearby with which to record the insights and lessons you learn during your time of fasting. It is sure to be a time of great blessing.

SIMPLY SPEAKING

Your hunger will serve as a call to prayer. It will remind you of your physical life, but your abstinence in the name of God will declare your avowed belief in the supremacy of the spiritual over the physical.

AUTHOR UNKNOWN

LIVING THE GOD LIFE

If you are not yet ready to give up food and water in a fast, why not try abstaining from something small like chocolate? Your sacrifice—however minor—will help to draw you closer to God and hear His voice more clearly.

BELIEVE—EVEN WHEN YOU DON'T SEE.

Jesus told him, "Because you have seen me, you have believed; blessed are those who have not seen and yet have believed."

JOHN 20:29

Throughout His ministry on earth, Jesus attracted enormous crowds because He did what no one else could: He gave sight to the blind and enabled the lame to walk. He fed five thousand men with only five loaves and two fishes. (Counting the women and children who were also present, the number was much higher.) And most amazing, Jesus even raised his friend Lazarus from the dead.

As long as He worked miracles before their eyes, people placed their faith in Jesus. But then He was nailed to the cross, and their hopes were shattered. Even Jesus' closest followers doubted His claim that He would overcome death and rise from the grave three days later. Thus, they returned to the lives they knew before they met Jesus.

Believing Jesus is alive and actively involved in our lives comes much more naturally when life works for us. We need no faith because no faith is required.

But how do you respond when life doesn't work for you?

Do you believe that Jesus exists, that He loves you, that He's still in control? Like many of Jesus' followers in His day, are you tempted to return to the life you knew before Jesus?

Do you need to see God's daily intervention in your life in order to trust Him? Real faith, the kind of faith that pleases God and helps us grow closer to Him, means believing that Jesus is at work in our lives—even when we don't see. Every challenge we face presents an opportunity to either rely on Jesus and believe that He is at work or rely on ourselves and live as if He doesn't exist.

Rather than live according to what you see, trust Jesus with your life, even when you don't see.

SIMPLY SPEAKING

Faith is to believe what you do not yet see: the reward for this faith is to see what you believe.

SAINT AUGUSTINE OF HIPPO

☺ LIVING THE GOD LIFE

*W*hat things is God asking you to believe—even though you can't see the results yet? How can you learn to trust Him more?

LEARN TO THINK LIKE A SERVANT.

*[Jesus said,] The greatest among you should be like the youngest,
and the one who rules like the one who serves. For who is greater,
the one who is at the table or the one who serves? Is it not the one who
is at the table? But I am among you as one who serves.*

LUKE 22:26–27

If Jesus were to appear to you in bodily form and ask you to
place someone else's interests before your own, how would you
respond?

Human nature tells us to "get there first with the most." All
things being equal, we like to stand at the front of the potluck
line. (If you wait too long, you may get stuck eating only Aunt
Rose's three-bean salad.) We would also like for someone else
to do the cleanup afterward. The thought of people putting our
needs first seems to be the life we prefer.

But stand in the back of the line? Clean up someone else's
mistakes? Wait on others? Are you kidding?

Serving others just doesn't come naturally. Jesus' disciples
bristled at the thought. In fact two of His disciples, James and
John, tried to convince Jesus to allow them to sit on His right and
left (the places of power and authority) in the coming kingdom.

Jesus, on the other hand, didn't seek to be served. The Son of

God left the comforts of heaven, came to earth, clothed Himself in human skin, and gave His life for us. He embodied the definition of servanthood.

And today, Jesus reveals Himself through us whenever we choose to serve others. To the extent that you serve the last and the least around you, you serve Jesus. Every time you step to the back of the line, clean up someone else's mistake, or prefer someone over yourself, you're really doing it for Jesus.

If you want to know Jesus, learn to think like a servant. Place other people's interests before your own, and you'll discover that you're in the company of Jesus Himself.

SIMPLY SPEAKING

God said: The higher they are in heaven, the more humble they are in themselves, and the closer to Me and the more in love with Me.

BROTHER LAWRENCE

 LIVING THE GOD LIFE

To whom can you be a servant today?

SIT BY THE BED OF A DYING CHRISTIAN.

None of us lives to himself alone and none of us dies to himself alone.
If we live, we live to the Lord; and if we die, we die to the Lord. So,
whether we live or die, we belong to the Lord.

ROMANS 14:7–8

Our culture has taught us to fear death. Images of the Grim
Reaper haunt our dreams and fill us with fright. Even those who
have given their lives to God are apprehensive at times: What
mystery lies beyond the veil? What's waiting on the other side
of our last breath? The best way to find out may be something
you've never considered. Simply sit by the bed of a dying
Christian and pay attention.

Those who have done so usually come away changed,
strengthened in faith, and inspired to live their lives with
greater hope and security. Sometimes they've seen arms
reach out for loved ones hidden from their sight. Perhaps
they've heard words heralding entrance of a saint into a
world he or she has only imagined. They may have seen
smiles and heard shouts of wonder. They've probably noticed
a lack of struggle and anxiety. And they've learned that dying
as a Christian is not dying at all. It is instead being ushered

into the land of promise—eternal life with God.

Our communion with God here on earth is sweet, but it isn't complete. Not until the day we close our human eyes for the last time and open our spiritual eyes to see Him in all His splendor and glory will we really know Him. At that moment, we will find no Grim Reaper, only a chorus of angelic voices and joy unspeakable.

Don't waste your time fearing death. Secure your eternal future through faith in Jesus Christ and look forward to the day when your faith will give way to sight, a day when you will be in the physical presence of your loving heavenly Father and your Lord Jesus. You will be closer to God than you could ever be here on earth.

SIMPLY SPEAKING

The fear of death is engrafted in the common nature of all men, but faith works it out of Christians.

VAVASOR POWELL

☺ LIVING THE GOD LIFE

What Christians do you know who have gone on to be with the Lord? What can you learn from their lives and faith?

DEAL WITH YOUR DOUBTS.

*Let us hold unswervingly to the hope we profess,
for he who promised is faithful.*

HEBREWS 10:23

What are your greatest doubts concerning God? Do you
ever wrestle with believing His relentless love or mighty power
reaches all the way to you? Do you wonder if He really sees you?
Do you question His goodness, justice, or even His existence?

If you do, you're in good company! Many great men and
women of faith in the Bible wrestled with doubts just as you
do. While running for his life from Queen Jezebel's troops, the
prophet Elijah doubted God's power to save him. In a troubling
moment, King David cried out, "My God, my God, why have
you forsaken me?" (Psalm 22:1). Martha, one of Jesus' closest
followers, doubted Jesus' ability to overcome death and the grave.

Often when we wrestle with doubt, we feel ashamed and try
to hide it. We convince ourselves that we're the only ones to feel
this way. We stuff it inside, hoping our doubt will go away. But it
doesn't.

If you wrestle with doubt, deal with it. Bring it out into the
open. Find people who are a little farther down the path than
you are and share it with them. They will be glad to help you talk

it through because they've been there. And in the process, two people will be encouraged and strengthened.

Doubt never goes away completely, but that's all right. True faith is born out of doubt because faith can exist only where God's love, power, goodness, or justice isn't readily seen. We need some doubt because as we deal with it, it facilitates our faith.

SIMPLY SPEAKING

Unless we start with doubts we cannot have a deep-rooted faith. One who believes lightly and unthinkingly has not much of a belief. He who has a faith which is not to be shaken has won it through blood and tears—has worked his way from doubt to truth as one who reaches a clearing through a thicket of brambles and thorns.

HELEN KELLER

😊 LIVING THE GOD LIFE

What doubts have you been secretly harboring in your heart? Bring them to God and allow His Spirit to fill you with the assurance you need to fully trust in Him.

ACCEPT THE FACT THAT GOD ACCEPTS YOU.

[God] chose us in Him before the foundation of the world . . .
according to the good pleasure of His will, to the praise of the glory of
His grace, by which He made us accepted in the Beloved.

EPHESIANS 1:4–6 NKJV

Peter denied Jesus three times. After witnessing His crucifixion and subsequent resurrection, the guilt overwhelmed him. How could Peter—a disciple of Jesus who served in His inner circle of three men—face the man he betrayed? And how could Jesus ever accept him again?

Many of us ask the same questions. Like Peter, all of us deny Jesus through our actions, words, thoughts, and intentions. Then the guilt of our sin overwhelms us, and we question whether our relationship with Him will ever be repaired.

The quick fix to the problem is to work harder. By doing good to other people, many of us hope that God will take us back and ignore our sin. But how do we know when we have done enough? Earning God's love and acceptance can be exhausting!

When Peter and Jesus finally discussed the betrayal, Peter encountered only one response from Jesus—love. Jesus didn't scold him or exhort him to do better, to try harder next time.

He simply encouraged Peter to do what he had done before the betrayal: follow Jesus and feed His sheep.

God loves you with an everlasting love. He loved you before the foundations of the earth were laid, and He'll love you after this present world comes to an end—and for eternity. If you can earn God's love and acceptance, then you can lose it as well. But if God loves and accepts you because He created you, because His nature is love, then you can do nothing to lose it. Give up your striving and rest in this priceless gift from your Creator.

SIMPLY SPEAKING

You are not accepted by God because you deserve to be, or because you have worked hard for him; but because Jesus died for you.

COLIN URQUHART

☺ **LIVING THE GOD LIFE**

God accepts you—just as you are. Thank Him today that you are one of His children, that nothing you could ever do will separate you from His love.

BECOME A WORLD-CLASS CHRISTIAN.

I pray that you may be active in sharing your faith, so that you will
have a full understanding of every good thing we have in Christ.

PHILEMON 1:6

People tend to define God by their own experiences. In
North America, we see God's faithfulness as we commute each
day, study hard at universities, or attempt to pay our mortgages.
But in other parts of the world Christians may see God at work
in bringing rain when there is a famine or protecting them from
civil unrest. God is interested in revealing Himself to all people
groups in ways that are meaningful to them.

So one way to draw closer to Him is to adopt His worldview.
As we see Jesus at work in ways that transcend our experience,
we discover that many sincere followers of Jesus worship much
differently than we do. We see physical needs that surpass our
own. We witness spiritual longings that come in different shapes
and sizes but can be filled only by Jesus. And we realize that God
may be calling us to join Him in His work.

God's involvement in this world isn't limited to our
hemisphere. He involves Himself in every race, culture, language,
and person. Witnessing God at work in the world around us
exposes us to His greatness.

Here are a few ideas to help you become a world-class Christian:

- Read magazines and books that describe what God is doing around the world.
- Pray for missionaries who serve in other countries—and pray for the countries where they serve.
- Involve yourself in a local outreach that ministers to people from cultures different from your own.
- Take a short-term mission trip sponsored by your church or a mission organization.

As your eyes are opened, you'll never want to go back to the small world you once inhabited.

Are you ready to discover how big your God is?

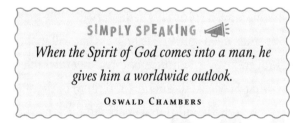

SIMPLY SPEAKING
When the Spirit of God comes into a man, he gives him a worldwide outlook.

OSWALD CHAMBERS

☺ LIVING THE GOD LIFE

*I*nvestigate exciting ways to participate in God's work throughout the earth. Sponsor a child in India or an orphanage in China. Support a missionary in Peru. Whatever you do, it will open your eyes to God's wider plan—and you will be richly blessed as a result!

READ AN INSPIRATIONAL BOOK.

Whatever things were written before were written for our learning,
that we through the patience and comfort of the Scriptures
might have hope.

ROMANS 15:4 NKJV

Exercise really doesn't make sense. When you think about it, shouldn't exercise deplete our bodies of energy? And shouldn't inactivity conserve them, giving us added energy? Oddly enough, taxing our lungs and our muscles depletes our energy in the short run but actually supplies additional energy in the long run.

In the same way, a spiritually sedentary lifestyle makes us weaker. Our souls need spiritual exercises that will make us stronger. Prayer, fasting, solitude, and reading the Bible are a few "workouts" that may cost us energy (and time) in the short run, but they supply us with additional energy in the long run. One easily overlooked spiritual exercise is reading a good book—one that inspires us to persevere in our spiritual journeys and encourages us to be all that God has called us to be.

Inspirational books can challenge our assumptions, expose us to new perspectives on God, and equip us to faithfully follow Christ. They can pull us out of our spiritual ruts and push us beyond our comfort zones. Most importantly, they can feed our hungry souls.

If you want to read an inspirational book but don't know where to start, ask spiritually mature people you respect for advice. Peruse the aisles of a Christian bookstore and look for titles that strike your fancy. Ask yourself, *What longings deep inside are making me spiritually hungry?*

Don't just pick up a book that you know will tell you what you already believe. Read a book that will challenge and stretch you. Broaden your understanding of the God who loves you, knows you, and desires to be known and loved by you.

As you do, you'll discover that you're giving yourself a spiritual workout. Best of all, you'll benefit from the added energy that spiritual exercise brings.

SIMPLY SPEAKING 📣

The things you read will fashion you by slowly conditioning your mind.

A. W. TOZER

☺ LIVING THE GOD LIFE

*I*s there a challenging or inspirational book that you've been longing to read? Why not take some time to pick it up and begin reading today?

ASK YOURSELF, *WHAT WOULD JESUS DO?*

[Jesus said,] I have set you an example that you should do as I have done for you.

JOHN 13:15

Every day we face hundreds, perhaps even thousands, of choices. Most decisions—like choosing which cereal to eat in the morning—affect no one and could be classified as neither right nor wrong. But every day we make a few decisions that affect us and the people around us. We don't remember our many insignificant choices, but the few significant choices we make can remain with us all day, keep us up at night, and at times, alter our lives.

How do we respond to difficult people? When do we speak our minds or keep silent? Do we give money to the homeless person standing on the street corner?

Whether you're sure or unsure what to do, the best place to begin is by asking yourself, *What would Jesus do?* He is the one person who never made a wrong choice and always fulfilled the will of His Father.

Read through the Gospels (Matthew, Mark, Luke, and John) and observe Jesus' life. What did Jesus do? He pointed people to

His Father in heaven and refused to allow His busy schedule to get in the way of their relationship. He spoke the truth in love. He healed the physical and spiritual needs of people around Him. And He gave His life away to others, even to seemingly insignificant people. Ultimately, Jesus' life led to the cross.

How can you live like Jesus? Acknowledge that you cannot live like Him on your own. Invite Him to live His life through you. Then ask yourself with each significant choice, *What would Jesus do?*

SIMPLY SPEAKING 📢

The whole idea of belonging to Christ is to look less and less like we used to and more and more like Him.

ANGELA THOMAS

☺ LIVING THE GOD LIFE

*I*n what situations of your life do you need to act more like Jesus?

HONOR YOUR FATHER AND MOTHER.

The command says, "Honor your father and mother." This is the first command that has a promise with it—"Then everything will be well with you, and you will have a long life on the earth."

EPHESIANS 6:2–3 NCV

Only one of the Ten Commandments directly addresses our behavior in the family—the fifth commandment, which tells us to honor our fathers and mothers. Now why would God include honoring our fathers and mothers on His Top-Ten list, alongside His mandates against murder, stealing, lying, and adultery?

We are who we truly are when we are with our families. In the workplace, at church, or any other time we are in public, we can fool people into believing that we have it all together. But when we're with family, our true colors shine through. Our families accept us often despite our behavior, not because of it.

The way we treat our families, especially our parents, reveals who we really are. Our behavior toward our fathers and mothers, who represent God's authority in our lives, exposes our view of authority—including God's. Similar to God, through your father and mother you were brought into this world. Without them (and your heavenly Father), you wouldn't be here.

To honor means to take someone seriously or to treat a

person with respect. What does it mean, then, to honor our fathers and mothers? It means:

- Responding to them with love (sometimes despite their behavior, not because of it).
- Listening to them.
- Spending time with them.
- Caring for them when they are older and unable to care for themselves.

Doesn't this resemble the way God responds to us? You may have grown up with abusive or mostly absent parents—what do you do then? Obviously you aren't obligated to honor them for their neglect or abuse, but you can still treat them with respect. Don't do it for them; do it for God.

Do you want to live a life that is honoring to God? Then begin by honoring your parents.

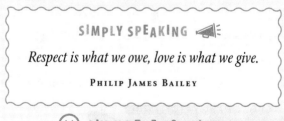

SIMPLY SPEAKING

Respect is what we owe, love is what we give.

PHILIP JAMES BAILEY

LIVING THE GOD LIFE

In what way can you actively honor and respect your parents today? Maybe a phone call, a card, or even a visit would express your appreciation for all that they have done for you.

SHOW RESPECT FOR THE PLANET.

*God blessed them and said to them, "Be fruitful and increase in
number; fill the earth and subdue it. Rule over the fish of the sea
and the birds of the air and over every living creature that
moves on the ground."*

GENESIS 1:28

When God created the heavens and the earth, He paid
special attention to the minutest details of His creation. He spent
the first four days focusing on the celestial bodies above, the
earth below, and vegetation. On the fifth day He created animals
that fly in the air and swim in the earth's oceans, lakes, rivers,
and streams. And on the sixth day of creation, after creating
animals that walk the earth, He fashioned Adam. As descendents
of Adam, we represent God's greatest achievement. No other
creature is created in the image of God and given a soul.

With that position in regard to the rest of creation, God has
also given us responsibility. We are to care for the earth and
all the resources we have been entrusted with. Isn't that what
any loving parent would expect after giving his or her child an
extraordinary gift? In just the same way, we are to take care of
what we've been given.

The Bible makes it clear that we are not to worship the earth or anything in it. We are always to worship only the Creator and live with respect and appreciation for Him. That means doing what we are able to do to avoid pollution of the air and water, the waste of natural resources, and the thoughtless destruction of wildlife.

God has given us a planet so magnificent that even He—the God of the universe—looked at it and pronounced it "good." We grow closer to Him when we treat what He has given us with care and understanding.

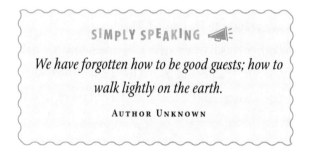

SIMPLY SPEAKING

We have forgotten how to be good guests; how to walk lightly on the earth.

AUTHOR UNKNOWN

☺ LIVING THE GOD LIFE

ℛealize that you are a steward of this beautiful planet you call home. What are some things you can do to become a better steward of what He has entrusted to you?

BE WILLING TO WALK THE SECOND MILE.

Give freely and spontaneously. Don't have a stingy heart. The way you handle matters like this triggers GOD, your God's, blessing in everything you do, all your work and ventures.

DEUTERONOMY 15:10 MSG

Jesus never asked the minimum from people who wanted to follow Him. He asked the maximum. He told the rich young ruler to give away everything He owned. He challenged His followers to turn the other cheek when struck by an enemy, to make gifts rather than loans. If someone asked for a coat, they were to give the person two coats. And if someone forced them to walk a mile, Jesus said they should walk two.

Walking the second mile means going beyond what is obligated, asked, or expected. It reveals the state of the heart. Although people can do good things with less-than-noble intentions, walking the second mile springs from God-honoring intentions and reveals the presence of grace, selflessness, and heavenly priorities.

Walking the second mile means giving your life away without expecting anything in return. You don't do it for yourself or another person; you do it for Jesus. Jesus taught that people who try to save their lives will lose them, but people who lose their lives for His sake will save them. You cannot give your life away without forgetting about yourself.

Of course, Jesus never asks of us what He isn't willing to give. He gave His life away for us by dying on the cross for our sins when He had no sin of His own.

Walking with Jesus means being willing to walk the second mile. You walk with Jesus when you:

- Give until it hurts.
- Forgive without being given an apology.
- Show compassion when you've had a bad day.
- Help others when you'd rather be doing something else.

Jesus is inviting you to walk the second mile with Him. Will you join Him?

SIMPLY SPEAKING

He who gives what he would as readily throw away, gives without generosity; for the essence of generosity is in self-sacrifice.

SIR HENRY TAYLOR

☺ LIVING THE GOD LIFE

*H*ow can you "walk the second mile" today?

LIVE ALL YOUR MOMENTS.

All the days ordained for me were written in your book
before one of them came to be.

PSALM 139:16

The Bible says that all our days, all our moments, were given
to us by God before we were even conceived. Imagine that! Each
tick of the clock is a gift, each heartbeat a glorious celebration.
Unfortunately, we tend to take our moments for granted. We
acknowledge, remember, appreciate only those moments that
grab our attention—moments of exhilaration, achievement,
passion, and celebration. We see His hand in the graduation
days, the wedding days, and the birthdays, but do we see Him in
the regular days, the workdays, the moments and hours that pass
almost without notice?

The interesting thing is that God is often found in the more
serene moments of our lives, those we pass off as mundane. Far
from the distractions of our high-profile moments, He whispers
in our ears, "Come closer, My child."

These moments are precious for the souls that wish to grow
closer to God—opportunities to add depth and dimension
to their spiritual lives. They are nurtured in the quiet of the
everyday.

Take care to cherish all your moments—every one. While you can't be consciously aware of every tick of the clock, you can be always listening, ready to open your heart to Him, always expecting that precious whisper assuring you that He is always near.

This moment—this very moment—you can grow closer to God simply by being available and inviting Him to share it with you. Live all your moments. Life is too precious to waste a single one.

SIMPLY SPEAKING

Wherever you are, be all there. Live to the hilt every situation you believe to be the will of God.

JIM ELLIOT

LIVING THE GOD LIFE

What is God saying to you in this very moment?

ONE WORD: *RELATIONSHIP.*

I think that all things are worth nothing compared with the greatness
of knowing Christ Jesus my Lord. . . . I want to know Christ and the
power that raised him from the dead.

PHILIPPIANS 3:8, 10 NCV

In the beginning, before the foundations of the world were
laid, before the stars were hung in the sky or anything else
existed, God lived in a relationship. God the Father, Son, and
Holy Spirit communed with one another, loved one another,
enjoyed one another.

Out of the mutual relationship they shared, they formed
the universe and then created the earth. And for their crowning
achievement, they molded the dust of the earth into the shape of
a human being and breathed life into its inanimate body.

The Bible tells us that God created Adam in His image. As
descendents of Adam, we're created in the image of God—not
that we look like Him, because the Father and the Holy Spirit
have no bodies. We're created in the image of God in that we
were given emotions and souls, and we were wired with the need
for a relationship—the kind shared by the Father, Son, and Holy
Spirit.

You were created for relationships. In the fabric of your

being, God wired you to share your life with others—to know
and be known. Isolation and emotional distance point to an
image in need of adjustment or repair.

But don't forget that you are God's crowning achievement.
He yearns to live in a relationship with you, and His ultimate
plan for you is to share a relationship with Him: communing
with one another, loving one another, enjoying one another. He
wants you to know *about* Him, but far more, He wants you to
know Him. You were created for a relationship with Him.

How do you deepen your relationship? Learn all you
can about Him. But more than that, look for Him, listen for
Him, enjoy Him, worship Him. He's waiting for you. Will you
respond?

SIMPLY SPEAKING

God and man exist for each other and neither is
satisfied without the other.

A. W. TOZER

☺ LIVING THE GOD LIFE

How strong is your relationship with God?
What things could you do to bring about a deeper and more
intimate walk with Him?

LIVE FOR OTHERS.

Each of you should look not only to your own interests,
but also to the interests of others.

PHILIPPIANS 2:4

When we live for ourselves, our world becomes small
because it extends only to whatever affects us. We care for others
if we think they will care for us. We help others if they might be
of some help in the future. The needs of others have little or no
bearing on us since they inhabit worlds outside of ours. The goal
of living for self is self-preservation. Ironically, Jesus said that
when we try to save our lives, we end up losing them. The Bible
calls this "living according to the flesh" (see Rom. 8:13 NKJV).

Living for others pulls us out of our small-minded worlds
and opens our eyes to the bigger world around us. When we
live for others, we forget about our problems and ultimately our
"selves." Without our "selves" getting in the way, we care without
being concerned about others caring for us and we help without
thought of receiving anything in return.

Jesus lived His life solely for others. He cared, He helped, He
loved, He gave—all without expectation of anything in return.
Rather than protecting Himself through self-preservation, He
offered Himself on a cross. Through His selfless life, death, and

subsequent resurrection, we receive the gift of salvation.

If you want to live for others, forget about your "self."
Don't worry about other people taking care of you, just give
your life away. If you find a need, fill it. If you see someone in
pain, soothe it. As you live for others, you begin to resemble
Jesus and discover that you're joining Him in giving your life
away. If you want to find Jesus, live for others, because that's
where He can be found.

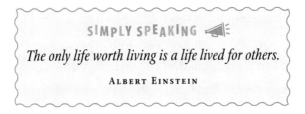

SIMPLY SPEAKING

The only life worth living is a life lived for others.

ALBERT EINSTEIN

☺ LIVING THE GOD LIFE

Who needs your help today? Give freely of your time,
your resources, your very self—and watch God reward you in
ways you never expected!

LOSE YOURSELF IN WORSHIP.

You alone are the LORD. *You made the heavens, even the highest*
heavens, and all their starry host, the earth and all that is on it,
the seas and all that is in them. You give life to everything, and the
multitudes of heaven worship you.

NEHEMIAH 9:6

Have you ever fallen in love? You can't sleep, you can't eat,
you can't concentrate. All you can think about is the other person
and what he or she is doing, eating, and thinking. You ache when
the two of you are apart and when you're together, no one else
matters because you find yourselves lost in one another. You
practically worship that person.

Did you know that God longs for the same kind of relationship with you? He's enraptured with you and His desire is
that you would be enraptured with Him. He wants you to lose
yourself in Him, to love Him with everything that is within you.
He wants to be the single focus of your life.

If you want to grow closer to God, lose yourself in
worship. When you spend time with Him at church or
elsewhere, try to shut out all distractions and focus solely
on Him. Free yourself from the constraints of time by
leaving your wristwatch at home. Forget about yourself, the

people around you, or the long list of tasks that you need to complete.

Then allow yourself to be in love with God. If you're singing a song or reading Scripture, reflect on the words as if God were speaking them to you. Pray as if God were hanging on to every word you speak. Imagine that He is using every detail of your life to woo you closer to Him—because He is.

SIMPLY SPEAKING 📢

It is only when men begin to worship that they begin to grow.

CALVIN COOLIDGE

☺ LIVING THE GOD LIFE

Why not spend some time today with God away from the distractions of life? Begin to worship Him for all that He is and all that He has done for you. Draw near to Him in worship— and He will draw near to you.

GREET THE "FELLOW" IN FELLOWSHIP.

Love the brothers and sisters of God's family.

1 PETER 2:17 NCV

Imagine yourself as a young child. Your family just moved into the neighborhood, you still haven't met anyone, and it's your first day at your new school. As you walk into the classroom, what runs through your head? *Look at all those strange faces. I wonder if anyone will like me, if I'll make any friends. I feel so alone.*

Every week, people walk into churches and feel the same way. Although they're grown up, adults often feel like children when they enter a church for the first time (or even after their first visit). They look around and see strange faces. They wonder if any of the people they see would make good friends. And they feel so alone.

Scripture urges us to welcome others as Christ has welcomed us. How have we been welcomed? We were:

- Loved without measure.
- Accepted unconditionally, regardless of our sin-stained condition.
- Invited to walk with Christ for the rest of our lives.
- Grafted into the family of God.

The next time you see an unfamiliar face at church, greet the person. Without being overbearing, make him or her feel welcome. Introduce other friends to your new friend. Offer to sit with the person in church. Invite him or her into your home or out to dinner.

You may need to depart from your comfortable surroundings, but don't forget that Christ left the comforts of heaven to welcome you into His kingdom. By extending yourself, you're entering into the ministry of Christ.

Greet the "fellow" in fellowship. At one time, you needed to be greeted, and God welcomed you with open arms.

SIMPLY SPEAKING

Those who dispel the loneliness and isolation
of others dispel those things in their
own lives as well.

ANDREA GARNEY

☺ LIVING THE GOD LIFE

Who needs your welcoming smile today?

PURSUE YOUR HEART'S PASSION.

May [God] grant you according to your heart's desire,
And fulfill all your purpose.

PSALM 20:4 NKJV

What makes your heart come alive? Some people pursue
their hearts' passions through art or music. Others find it by
working on cars or playing with children. Still others never
pursue their hearts' passions and live with a dull, aching sense
that something is missing.

In the movie *Chariots of Fire*, Olympic track-and-field gold
medalist Eric Liddell commented about his running, "God
made me fast, and when I run, I feel His pleasure." Through his
running, Eric Liddell pursed his heart's desire.

The Westminster Catechism, a widely accepted summary
of Christian belief, states that the chief end of man is to "glorify
God and enjoy Him forever." Was Eric Liddell enjoying God
while he ran? Yes. Was God being glorified? Absolutely! By
doing what God created him to do, Eric Liddell transformed his
running into an act of worship.

You know you're pursing your heart's passion when you feel
exhilarated, motivated, and alive. Pursuing your heart's passion
frees you to become who you really are. The vestiges of the

person society forces you to be fall off, and you express yourself as you truly are. As your heart comes alive, you find that the vestiges that hinder your relationship with God fall off as well. Your heart's passion then becomes an opportunity for worship.

If you aren't sure what your heart's passion looks like, here are a few questions to ask yourself:

- What am I good at?
- What do other people say I'm good at?
- What do I enjoy doing?
- When do I feel most alive?

By pursuing your heart's passion, you experience the life God specifically designed for you. And best of all, through it you glorify and enjoy God and feel His pleasure.

SIMPLY SPEAKING

Each one of us has a fire in our heart for something. It's our goal in life to find it and keep it.

MARY LOU RETTON

☺ LIVING THE GOD LIFE

What is your heart's passion? What did God create you—and only you—to do?

REJOICE IN GOD'S MERCY.

The LORD your God is a merciful God; he will not abandon or destroy you or forget the covenant with your forefathers, which he confirmed to them by oath.

DEUTERONOMY 4:31

Ever since Adam and Eve disobeyed God in the Garden of Eden, we have given Him plenty of opportunities to show us mercy. God chose not to destroy Adam and Eve when they ate the forbidden fruit. Later, during Israel's forty-year wandering in the desert, they worshiped foreign gods at the very moment God gave them the Ten Commandments through Moses. Nevertheless, He chose not to destroy His chosen people and start over again. Centuries later, when Jesus was nailed to a cross on trumped-up charges, God still refused to destroy all humankind.

If we're honest with ourselves, our lives bear an uncomfortable resemblance to those of our predecessors. Through our thoughts and actions, we disobey God, worship foreign gods, and nail Jesus to the cross all over again. Yet God still showers His mercy on us by offering us forgiveness and eternal life.

Mercy means not giving someone what he or she deserves. When someone hurts you and you refuse to retaliate but instead forgive, that's an act of mercy. The most common Hebrew word for mercy means "steadfast love." It's a love that refuses to give up, despite actions that push that love away.

In the book of Lamentations, the writer refers to God's mercies as "new every morning" (3:23). Every day, God shows us new depths of His mercy. He involves Himself in our everyday lives. He refuses to punish us according to what we deserve and even offers us eternal life. He does it not because we deserve it, but because He loves us. And that is the greatest gift of all.

SIMPLY SPEAKING 📢

God's mercy is boundless, free and, through Jesus Christ our Lord, available to us now in our present situation.

A. W. TOZER

☺ LIVING THE GOD LIFE

When you wake up tomorrow morning, think of all the ways God has shown you His mercy. Rejoice in it!

ASK FOR WISDOM.

If any of you lacks wisdom, he should ask God, who gives generously to all without finding fault, and it will be given to him.

JAMES 1:5

How often do you face a decision that leaves you unsure how to respond? You go with what you think is best, and sometimes the decision seems to work out. But how do you really know if you made the right decision? Fortunately, you can always ask God for wisdom.

Human wisdom tends to operate within the limits of what we can see. It can't help but spring from our earthly perspective because our only basis for wisdom comes from personal experience. Relying on ourselves for advice, then, naturally drives our decisions toward self-interest and self-preservation. Asking others for advice often gives us more of the same.

God's wisdom, however, differs greatly from ours. Since God lives in eternity, His wisdom springs from an eternal perspective—a perspective that sees every side of every issue (especially God's side). The Bible tells us that the wisdom from God is pure, peaceable, gentle, open to reason, "full of mercy and good fruit, impartial and sincere" (James 3:17).

Regardless of the scope of the decision you may be facing,

spend time in prayer asking God for wisdom. Ask other believers to pray for you or with you. God promises to share His wisdom with anyone who asks—in generous amounts. Don't worry about whether or not you deserve it; He will grant you the wisdom you need without scolding you or pointing out your faults.

How do you know when God has given you His wisdom? Often you don't. Sometimes His wisdom looks like a decision you would make, other times it doesn't. But this much you can know: His wisdom is all you will ever need to get it right every time.

SIMPLY SPEAKING

Men may acquire knowledge, but wisdom is a gift direct from God.

BOB JONES

☺ LIVING THE GOD LIFE

*I*n what situations of your life do you most need God's wisdom? He gives it freely to those who ask. Why not ask Him for it today?

GLORY IN YOUR WEAKNESSES.

The Spirit helps us in our weakness.

ROMANS 8:26

You need help. No, really. We all need help. Unfortunately, we often fool ourselves into thinking that we have it all together. Society tells us to accentuate our strengths and minimize our weaknesses. So we look at our weaknesses with shame and do whatever we can to hide them. No matter how deep our denial, though, our weaknesses don't go away.

Did you know that your strengths are your greatest weakness and your weaknesses are your greatest strength? It's true.

The problem with thinking we have it all together is that it prevents us from seeing our need for God. We think we don't need God if we can handle life ourselves. And we give Him no room to work in our lives if we think we have no rooms that need work. *Self-sufficiency* is just another word for *pride*, and it pushes God away from us rather than drawing us closer.

So it's okay to express your fears, your hurts, your sins to others. It even encourages others to reach out for help as well.

Glory, rejoice, boast in your weaknesses. Let them remind you how insufficient you are and how sufficient God is. Reach out for His strength, comfort, compassion, and intervention.

Trust Him to use your weaknesses to make Himself real in your life.

Confess your sins and acknowledge your weaknesses not only to God, but to others. You'll be amazed at the many people who experience the same struggles you do. And you'll give God an opportunity to show His strength in your life.

SIMPLY SPEAKING

When God is our strength, it is strength indeed;
when our strength is our own, it is only weakness.

SAINT AUGUSTINE OF HIPPO

☺ LIVING THE GOD LIFE

What are your greatest weaknesses? How can God use those weaknesses to show Himself strong in your life?

LEARN THE SECRET OF CONTENTMENT.

I say it is better to be content with what little you have.
Otherwise, you will always be struggling for more,
and that is like chasing the wind.

ECCLESIASTES 4:6 NCV

What do you need to be happy? A big house? A nice car? An income that allows you to live extravagantly and take vacations to exotic places? As you probably already suspect, none of those things bring happiness. Most of us know it in our heads, but far fewer of us know it in our hearts.

Is happiness the goal of life? Perhaps from a temporal perspective, but not necessarily from God's. In our society, happiness usually refers to the sense of well-being and contentment that occurs when the various aspects of our lives come into harmony with one another. If we achieve our goals (especially financial), avoid pain and hardship, and maintain satisfying relationships, then we can claim to be happy. When life goes south, however, our sense of happiness dissolves like a Popsicle on a hot sidewalk. Because circumstances change, our sense of happiness does too.

Scripture, on the other hand, prescribes a different pursuit.

We're encouraged to pursue not happiness but an otherworldly contentment. Since this world is not our home, seeking satisfaction from it will always leave us unfulfilled—always. Our treasure lies in heaven, so the amount of our treasures here on earth means little. Our relationships in this life don't define us; our relationship with Christ does. So when our world is in disharmony, it's okay. This world isn't our home anyway.

The secret of contentment is found in the truth that when you have Jesus, you already have everything. You can handle conflict in your relationships when you are at peace in your relationship with Christ. And that will bring the greatest happiness you could ever know.

SIMPLY SPEAKING

Contentment is not the fulfillment of what you want, but the realization of how much you already have.

AUTHOR UNKNOWN

☺ LIVING THE GOD LIFE

Take an inventory of your life. Are you seeking happiness or contentment? Your answer will tell you where you're making your home.

MAINTAIN A LOW PROFILE.

Humble yourselves before the Lord, and he will lift you up.

JAMES 4:10

Deep inside, all of us hunger for recognition. Victory doesn't taste as sweet without a generous helping of accolades. Our accomplishments take on greater significance when recognized in front of our peers. We like to be thanked for our "selfless" contributions with big plaques inscribed with our names on them. And if we don't get recognized, we feel neglected or overlooked. So, we position ourselves in such a way that people see us.

The kingdom of God, however, operates with a completely different set of values than the kingdom of this world. Some people refer to it as the "upside-down kingdom" because it runs opposite of conventional wisdom.

Conventional wisdom tells us that if we don't blow our own horn, no one else will. We must promote ourselves at work or we may miss receiving a promotion or a pay raise. It's okay to strut our stuff if we can back it up.

The upside-down kingdom, on the other hand, values humility over self-promotion. The Bible tells us that God humbles the proud and exalts the humble. You don't need to blow your own horn because God will do it for you at the right time—when He knows you can handle it. Oftentimes, our desire to promote ourselves in subtle (or not-so-subtle) ways really masks a voracious appetite called pride. Humility draws us closer to God; pride drives us farther from Him.

Rather than promote yourself, maintain a low profile instead. Do good and be good at what you do—whether or not people are watching—and let God promote you. God is big enough and good enough that you can trust Him to promote you when He knows you're ready.

SIMPLY SPEAKING

The proud man counts his newspaper clippings—the humble man his blessings.

FULTON J. SHEEN

☺ LIVING THE GOD LIFE

When was the last time you did something good—without anyone watching?

THINK LIKE A GUEST RATHER THAN AN OWNER.

Be shepherds of God's flock that is under your care, serving as overseers—not because you must, but because you are willing, as God wants you to be; not greedy for money, but eager to serve; not lording it over those entrusted to you, but being examples to the flock.

1 PETER 5:2–3

Some people act as if they own the world. They expect preferential treatment when they eat at restaurants or go shopping. They talk about themselves incessantly. And they get irritable when they don't get their way. Don't people like that really bug you?

In reality, the "I own the world" mind-set plagues all of us—some of us just cover it up better than others. We like preferential treatment; we like talking about ourselves; and we get irritated (at least inwardly) when we don't get our way.

You would think that the person who really does own the world would act like an owner. But He didn't. When Jesus came to earth, He emptied Himself of the privileges of being God and became a guest, a stranger among us. Although the universe and everything in it were created by Him and for Him, He didn't ask for or expect preferential treatment. Instead, He looked after the needs of others—young, old, rich, poor, sick, and healthy. He forgot about Himself and carried out the ultimate act of humility by dying for everyone's sins on a cross. He gave everything but He owned nothing.

If you want to be like Jesus, think like a guest rather than an owner. Lay down your rights at the feet of the people around you. Forget about your needs, and look for ways to please God, who owns everything.

Without a heart change, you'll continually return to the owner mind-set. Ask God to give you a heart like Jesus. Ask Him to open your eyes to the people around you. And ask Jesus to bless others through you.

SIMPLY SPEAKING

The princes among us are those who forget themselves and serve mankind.

WOODROW WILSON

☺ LIVING THE GOD LIFE

*H*ow can you begin to think like a "guest" rather than an "owner"? By opening the door for a stranger? By letting the person behind you have the best parking place? By giving of yourself to help someone in need?

PRACTICE THE PRESENCE OF GOD.

The LORD your God goes with you;
he will never leave you nor forsake you.

DEUTERONOMY 31:6

When we say we want to grow closer to God, what do we really mean? Realistically, how can we grow closer to someone who already indwells us and fills all the world around us? What we really want to know—need to know—is how to become more consciously aware of His presence in our lives.

Here are some suggestions:

- Imagine the Lord standing or sitting next to you wherever you are. In fact, He is there—you are not imagining Him at all. Instead, you are acknowledging His presence.

- He goes where you go and sees what you see. Once you realize that He is with you no matter what, you will not want to go where you should not.

- Stop to consider that He is hearing every word you say and listening to everything that's said to you. You will find yourself avoiding gossip, profanity, and conversations that aren't pleasing to Him.

God is near you whether you are aware of Him or not. And if

you have given your heart to Him, He is more than nearby—He's dwelling within you. Determine to please Him first in everything you do. Honor Him by fleeing from temptation and staying out of situations where He is not respected or acknowledged. Life changes for good when you understand that God is your constant Companion.

SIMPLY SPEAKING 📢

Were I a preacher, I should preach above all other things the practice of the presence of God. Were I a teacher, I should advise all the world to it; so necessary do I think it, and so easy.

BROTHER LAWRENCE

☺ LIVING THE GOD LIFE

Why not talk to God throughout your day as you would a friend? There are times when you may need to find a place to pray more formally. But God is always with you and eager to listen to what you have to say—no matter where you are or what you are doing.

PAY ATTENTION TO THE NEEDS AROUND YOU.

Contribute to the needs of the saints; extend hospitality to strangers.

ROMANS 12:13 NRSV

Throughout the Gospels (Matthew, Mark, Luke, and John), Jesus appeared in the midst of pain, poverty, and suffering. People followed Him because He made the lame walk, healed the lepers, delivered the demonically oppressed, and gave sight to the blind.

Jesus not only met people's physical needs, He also met people's emotional and spiritual needs. During His ministry, Jesus was like a heat-seeking missile honed in on the needs of others. If you wanted to find Jesus, all you had to do was look around for a need, and He was probably there.

Jesus is still there.

If you want to find Jesus, if you want to serve Him, if you want to show Him how much you love Him, pay attention to the needs around you. Jesus said that every time you feed the hungry, give a drink to the thirsty, welcome a stranger, clothe the naked, or visit someone in prison, you do it unto Him. It's as if you are ministering to Jesus Himself.

When you look into the eyes of someone in need, you look

into the eyes of Jesus. What color are His eyes? The color of
sadness, loneliness, and pain. He wears old, ratty clothes and
pin-striped suits. He smells like the homeless man who wanders
the streets at night. And He lives next door in the stories your
neighbor is afraid to tell.

Take a moment to look around you. Jesus is everywhere.
Serve Him.

SIMPLY SPEAKING 📢

*God has so ordered that men, being in need of
each other, should learn to love each other, and
bear each other's burdens.*

GEORGE AUGUSTUS SALA

☺ LIVING THE GOD LIFE

Who needs you to demonstrate the love of Jesus to him
or her today?

ALWAYS GIVE GOD YOUR BEST.

It is God who arms me with strength and makes my way perfect.
He makes my feet like the feet of a deer; he enables me
to stand on the heights.

2 SAMUEL 22:33–34

God is awesome—great and mighty, all-knowing and always present, Creator and Conqueror. He reigns and rules over everything and everyone. When you look at all that, when you examine His glory, do you feel a little intimidated? Do you wonder how you can ever do anything to please a God like that? Like trying to choose the right gift for a billionaire, it seems like an exercise in futility.

Well . . . God is pleased—pleased with your effort to grow closer to Him in mind and spirit. And He does expect a lot of you, but never more than you are able to give. What He will ask you for is your best.

God knows you are not His equal. If you were, He would not be God. Trying to be perfect as God is perfect is not achievable for human beings. We sacrificed our ability to walk perfectly when we allowed sin into our lives. Instead, God is pleased when we give Him our all. He takes our best and stretches it, works it, strengthens it, and perfects it until it is precisely what is needed.

He crowns our efforts with His own perfection.

You will never grow close to God by trying to be perfect. Forget about it. You will fail every time and finally, you will give up and your opportunity for relationship with God will be lost. Promise instead that you will do your best, give Him all you have to give. Then trust Him to make your gift pleasing and your effort equal to the task.

SIMPLY SPEAKING

God demands perfection from his creatures, but if they will ever have it, he himself must supply it. We need not be concerned about how high God's standard is, as long as he meets it for us.

ERWIN W. LUTZER

☺ LIVING THE GOD LIFE

In what areas have you given God your best lately? In what areas do you still have room to grow?

SURRENDER YOUR PERSONAL PAIN.

*I consider that the sufferings of this present time are not worth
comparing with the glory about to be revealed to us.*

ROMANS 8:18 NRSV

Have you ever experienced a broken heart? A disappointment so severe that you felt you couldn't go on? Have you been
robbed of your happiness, crippled by shame, or victimized by
abuse? If so—and very few, if any, have not—you know what it is
to be in pain.

It really doesn't matter if the pain in your life is physical,
mental, or emotional. It can really knock you out of the game
if you let it. Does that surprise you? Have you ever imagined
that you have a choice? It would be misleading to pretend that
overcoming your pain would be easy. Clearly, it would mean
struggle and determination, but if you're willing, God can help
you move it from your path.

God doesn't like to see you in pain for any reason. But
more than that, He realizes that when you are focusing on
your broken heart, severe disappointment, loss of happiness,
heart full of shame, or the memory of abuse, you cannot
focus on Him. If you wish to grow closer to Him, you must be
willing to come out of hiding, surrender your personal pain

to Him, and get past it so you can put Him first.

As justified as your pain may be, it is still your pain. You have the power to leave it out where it will dog your thoughts and actions all day every day or leave it with Someone who can help you put it behind you and pursue a closer relationship with the One who never disappoints. You can be sure that He will never break your heart.

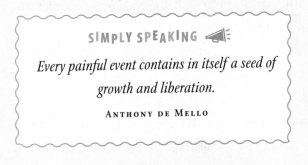

SIMPLY SPEAKING

Every painful event contains in itself a seed of growth and liberation.

ANTHONY DE MELLO

☺ LIVING THE GOD LIFE

Are you ready to turn to the One who loves you dearly? Why not pour out your heart to God, asking Him to take your hand and help you overcome your pain?

RUN FROM TEMPTATION.

Submit yourselves, then, to God. Resist the devil,
and he will flee from you.

JAMES 4:7

Some battles give you a fighting chance of winning. Others don't. And when you face a battle you know you can't win, you're best off running the other direction.

Temptation is one of those battles. Anytime you fight it, you stand a good chance of losing. The Bible warns us to flee sexual immorality, youthful passions, the worship of idols (anything that competes with our devotion to Christ), and the love of money. Rather than walk away, or stand there and look at it for a while, we're commanded to run from sin as if our lives depended on it. They do. Don't fight sin, fear it.

Why does God command us to run? Because the stakes are high. Satan, the enemy of our souls, fights dirty. He attacks us at our point of weakness and aims to neutralize our relationship with God. Although Satan cannot overcome God's overwhelming power, we're not God.

How do you run? If possible, you eliminate any temptation that lures you away from God's love—even if it requires changing your lifestyle. If you struggle with Internet porn, discontinue your service or purchase filtering software. If you're tempted to engage in an inappropriate relationship, discontinue the relationship. If you know that your love for money and the stuff money can buy is driving you deeper into debt, cut up your credit cards.

When you run from sin, what do you run to? You run to Christ and acknowledge your utter need for Him to intervene. But you also run to the body of Christ, the church. Share your temptations and failings with people who can walk beside you in your struggle. Resisting temptation can be harder to do in isolation.

Your soul is too valuable to be wounded by even frivolous skirmishes. So run from temptation.

SIMPLY SPEAKING

Little by little, with patience and fortitude, and with the help of God, you will sooner overcome temptations than with your own strength and persistence.

THOMAS À KEMPIS

☺ LIVING THE GOD LIFE

What are your greatest areas of temptation? What specific things can you do to overcome those temptations?

TEND YOUR INNER ORCHARD.

The fruit of the Spirit is love, joy, peace, patience, kindness, goodness, faithfulness, gentleness and self-control.

GALATIANS 5:22–23

Have you ever tried to make fruit grow on a tree? First you yank the seedling out of the ground. Then you massage the branches until a few small budding flowers form. Then you gently tug on the flowers until the fruit comes out.

Of course, none of that is true. You can't make fruit grow. All you can do is tend the tree by giving it the right amount of water, food, sunlight, and protection from danger.

The fruit of the Spirit works the same way. Love, joy, peace, patience, kindness, goodness, faithfulness, gentleness, and self-control don't just happen on their own. Nor can you produce them on your own.

The fruit of the Spirit is literally the evidence of the Holy Spirit's work in your life. Because you cannot control the Spirit, you cannot make the Spirit produce fruit in your life. However, you can tend your inner orchard.

Feed your inner orchard with generous helpings of God's Word. Don't just learn what it says, listen to what it says to you. Then water it with prayer. Ask God to weed out any influences that distract you from your relationship with Him and to mold you into the shining image of Christ. Don't forget to spend time listening to the voice of the Master Gardener. Next, protect the work God is doing in you by entering into relationships with other followers of Jesus. The deeper your relationships, the better the protection.

The result of tending your inner orchard is more than just the fruit of the Spirit growing in your life. You'll discover that you're becoming like Jesus, from whom the fruit springs.

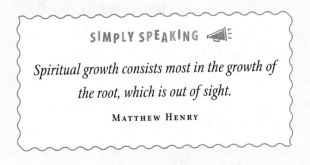

SIMPLY SPEAKING

Spiritual growth consists most in the growth of the root, which is out of sight.

MATTHEW HENRY

☺ **LIVING THE GOD LIFE**

Which fruit of the Spirit would you like to see more of in your life? As you allow the Master Gardener to help you tend your inner orchard, you'll be amazed at the bountiful harvest He will bring.

MARRY YOURSELF TO THE TRUTH.

[Jesus said,] I came into the world, to testify to the truth.
Everyone on the side of truth listens to me.

JOHN 18:37

Paul and Silas were traveling throughout Asia, preaching the gospel in local synagogues. One location, however, stood out among the rest. The people of Berea listened intently to Paul and Silas's words, but they also compared what they heard with what they read in Scripture. After determining that what they heard was true, they accepted Paul and Silas's message.

All of us are bombarded with different versions of truth. Especially in an individualistic society like ours, many people fashion it according to their tastes, experiences, and opinions. Cultures are particularly effective at establishing their versions of truth, which then permeate the lives of the people within them. Because cultures differ from one another, how do you discern right from wrong?

You marry yourself to the truth.

Only one resource offers timeless truth that transcends every person and every culture: God's Word. It shows us how to navigate our way through the myriad choices we face because it not only defines truth, it is truth.

If you want to marry yourself to the truth:

- Invite the Holy Spirit to guide you into all truth.
- Ask yourself, *Is my faith built on culture or Scripture?* Then evaluate your beliefs in light of God's Word.
- Allow Scripture to serve as the grid through which all information runs—whether it be the newspaper, a movie, or a sermon you hear in church. Accept as truth only what agrees with Scripture.

Marrying yourself to the truth means being committed to it regardless of the prevailing opinions at the time. You may disagree with it, it may force you to make unpopular decisions, you may even have to change your lifestyle. But by joining yourself to the truth, you join yourself to the One who is truth.

SIMPLY SPEAKING 📣

I think the most important quality in a person concerned with religion is absolute devotion to truth.

ALBERT SCHWEITZER

☺ LIVING THE GOD LIFE

Why not ask the Holy Spirit to illuminate truth to you as you study God's Word? When you allow the Scriptures to be the standard by which you judge everything around you, your life will be built on the solid rock of God's truth.

BE A DOER AND NOT A HEARER ONLY.

He who looks into the perfect law of liberty and continues in it,
and is not a forgetful hearer but a doer of the work, this one will be
blessed in what he does.

JAMES 1:25 NKJV

A few years ago a shoe company conducted an ad campaign with the theme "Just do it!" In scene after scene, the same well-known athlete embarked on different athletic adventures—from basketball to bobsledding. The campaign urged viewers to embark on different adventures of their own. Don't be afraid or reluctant, just do it—with their shoes, of course.

In the same way, Scripture encourages all of us to "Just do it!" Rather than allow fear or reluctance to mesmerize us into inactivity, we should embark on the great adventure of obeying God's Word.

Living in a society that worships at the altar of information often fools believers into assuming that mastering Bible facts makes us godly. But if we know what the Bible says and do nothing about it, we deceive ourselves into believing that knowledge is equivalent to godliness. Knowing what the Bible says about love and compassion doesn't necessarily make us loving and compassionate.

Scripture encourages us to train ourselves for godliness (see 1 Tim. 4:7). When we give our lives to Jesus, He makes us holy. But becoming godly—which means to become more like God— is a lifelong pursuit.

We must become doers of God's Word and not hearers only (see James 1:22 NKJV).

God transforms us when we put His Word into practice. Don't just read the Bible, do what it says. Don't just listen to inspiring messages about prayer, pray. Don't just read books about sharing your faith with others, share your faith.

When you become a doer of the Word, God begins forming the character of Jesus in you. He gives you the strength to be the person you couldn't be on your own. And you embark on the adventure of becoming a vessel God enjoys working through.

SIMPLY SPEAKING

God will never reveal more truth about himself till you obey what you know already.

OSWALD CHAMBERS

☺ LIVING THE GOD LIFE

As you read the Bible, consider ways in which you might apply each passage to your own life. How does God want you to change as a result of what you've studied? In what ways can you live out His Word in your daily walk with Him?

EMBRACE YOUR TRIALS.

Consider it pure joy, my brothers,
whenever you face trials of many kinds.

JAMES 1:2

How can you count trials as joys, as the Bible instructs? It seems contradictory, but good can come from trials. Their final outcome should show profit for you, not loss. That is something to rejoice over. You can learn from every struggle. View trials as opportunities rather than as obstacles.

Realize God is in control. Every circumstance in your life has been filtered through His hands. God desires only your very best. When He allows trials in your life, they are to help you grow and become a better person.

Sometimes God uses trials to test you—not so much to show your strength to Him, but to you. You might be surprised at how well you do on the test. Often the first response to a trial is, "God, please take this away!" Wouldn't it be better to ask Him, "What do You want me to gain from this experience? Please guide me as I go through it." Trials should draw you closer to God.

Strive to maintain a positive outlook while going through trials. You may need to spend time waiting on the Lord. God is not slow, and His timing is perfect. He will provide peace in the midst of your stormy waters. His Word also contains wise counsel and reassuring comfort.

Trials produce endurance and increase your faith. Successfully overcoming leads to maturity. You can use what you learn from these trials to encourage others when they go through similar times.

God may not tell you why you are experiencing trials, but He will always be there to help you during them.

SIMPLY SPEAKING

All our difficulties are only platforms for the manifestation of His grace, power, and love.

HUDSON TAYLOR

☺ LIVING THE GOD LIFE

Why not hand all your worries and fears over to the Lord? Be honest—tell Him exactly how you feel. And while you're talking, ask Him to help you joyfully embrace your trials.

EMERGE FROM YOUR RUT.

[Jesus said,] I tell you the truth, unless you change and become like little children, you will never enter the kingdom of heaven.

MATTHEW 18:3

Perhaps you have been living for God all your life. You've known Him since you were a child. You've memorized His Word and know firsthand what prayer and faith in God can do. You've experienced divine love, and you've known God's goodness in your life and the lives of those you love. Some people might look at you and say: "That person has all of God he [or she] will ever need." You agree that should be true, but the truth is you've stopped growing, lost your zeal. You're in a spiritual rut.

When you hit one of those places—and we all do—the best thing is to drop back and approach from another angle.

Here are a few ideas to renew your faith and help you grow closer to God—again:

- Read your Bible as if you were reading it for the first time. Sometimes breaking out of old patterns requires taking a new perspective. (Using a different translation of the Bible can help.)
- Pray, assuming that God really is listening. He is.

- Remind yourself that God is present in your everyday affairs.
- Expect that God is already acting on your behalf. Perhaps He's bigger than you thought and able to work outside the parameters of what you define as good. Maybe that's what makes Him God.

The wonderful thing about relationship—especially with God—is that it is a living thing. It moves and changes. Unless you change with it, always growing and experiencing God in new ways, you will land in a rut. It happens. Just climb out and brush yourself off. God is always ready to move on with you.

SIMPLY SPEAKING

If thou shalt remain faithful and zealous in labor, doubt not that God shall be faithful and bountiful in rewarding thee.

THOMAS À KEMPIS

☺ LIVING THE GOD LIFE

Ask God to give you new eyes today: Eyes that look for the divine in everyday living. Eyes that find miracles in ordinary situations. Eyes that view life with wonder and delight.

LIVE OUT IN THE OPEN.

You have preserved me because I was honest; you have admitted me
forever to your presence.

PSALM 41:12 TLB

Christians are supposed to have it all together. We shouldn't
struggle with anger, fear, lust, worry, or addictions, because our
lives are different, right? Wrong.

Once we become followers of Jesus, we become new
creations, but we are still left with the old bodies and emotions
so the struggle with sin continues. The good news, though, is that
Jesus has broken the power of sin over us and through the power
of His Holy Spirit, we can now resist sin.

But sometimes we feel that we should be perfect, so we try
and, of course, we fail. So out of fear of being discovered, we hide
our pains and sins and act as if everything's okay. As a result, we
become walking contradictions, proclaiming the abundant life
Jesus gives while we're dying inside.

Hiding our true selves only covers our pain and fosters our
sin. It never heals us, nor does it restore us because we cannot
overcome ourselves by ourselves. All of us need outside help.

How would you feel if you learned that other sincere
followers of Jesus shared similar pains and struggled with the

same kinds of sins as you? You'd probably feel relieved and encouraged. Well, it's true!

When we live out in the open, we expose our true selves. As we enter into authentic relationships with other believers, we discover that we aren't alone. Some people may be ahead of us in their recovery, others may follow behind. But together, we experience the comfort, healing, and restoration that can come only from Christ and through the body of Christ.

So live out in the open. You'll discover you aren't alone—and that Jesus is there to comfort, heal, and restore you.

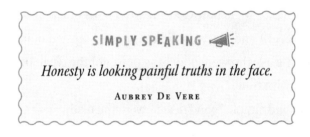

SIMPLY SPEAKING

Honesty is looking painful truths in the face.

AUBREY DE VERE

☺ LIVING THE GOD LIFE

With whom can you be open and honest about the struggles you are facing? As you begin to share your experiences with that person, you'll be amazed at the comfort and joy that living in the open can bring.

GO ABOUT DOING GOOD!

Who is wise and understanding among you? Let him show it by his
good life, by deeds done in the humility that comes from wisdom.

JAMES 3:13

The Bible says that while Jesus was here on earth, those who
traveled with Him—His disciples and other committed followers,
along with the crowds that listened to Him as He preached from
the mountainsides and along the seashore—saw Him doing
good. "You know . . . how God anointed Jesus of Nazareth with
the Holy Spirit and power, and how he went around doing good
and healing all who were under the power of the devil, because
God was with him" (Acts 10:37–38).

Pure and simple "good deeds" were the instruments Jesus
used to teach God's love and His plan of redemption. He fed the
hungry, healed the sick, opened the eyes of the blind, intervened
on behalf of the fallen, and even raised the dead. His compassion
is almost palpable as we read through the Gospels, seeing Jesus'
actions through the eyes of the gospel writers.

We have also been called to deliver good news—the news
that God loves us. We are His fallen creation but not His
forgotten creation. This news is often revealed to us in situations
where we see God's goodness in our lives: an answered prayer, a

new beginning, relief from suffering. His goodness points to His love. Shouldn't we follow His example by pointing people to God through acts of goodness?

Let others see God's love for them through you. Each time you reach out to someone in need, whether a friend or a stranger—you are showing God's love by doing good. It's God's way and that's always the best way.

SIMPLY SPEAKING

True Christianity is love in action.

DAVID O. MCKAY

😊 LIVING THE GOD LIFE

What "good deed" could you perform today?

ASK, SEEK, KNOCK.

[Jesus said,] Keep on asking, and you will be given what you ask for.
Keep on looking, and you will find. Keep on knocking,
and the door will be opened.

MATTHEW 7:7 NLT

How will you get an answer if you don't ask? How can you find if you don't seek? How can you expect the door to open if you do not knock?

In their original language, Jesus' words convey continuing action—keep asking, keep seeking, keep knocking. Be persistent.

Asking could be a question, a request, or an invitation. With confidence, ask the One who knows all and has all. Don't be concerned about repeatedly asking until the answer is clear. God doesn't get tired of you. But don't be arrogant and demanding either. Just ask simply and specifically, and look for the answer.

Seek, search, strive for, and you will find. You must actively go after what you seek. Sometimes God requires your action as part of His answering process.

Knock to be granted entrance. Don't try to force your way in. But don't knock only once and leave. Wait for the door to open. Keep knocking until it does.

Scripture offers examples of people who followed this

directive. God told King Solomon to ask for whatever he wanted and it would be granted. Jesus told His followers to pray in His name in order to receive. If you ask in faith and according to God's will, He will answer.

Even though God knows your every thought, He wants you to tell Him your requests. Whether aloud or in your mind, you must ask in order to receive. Seek to know and do God's will. *Knock* is another word for *ask* and *seek*. The Bible often uses patterns of three for emphasis.

Ask, seek, knock. Don't give up. God is ever ready to answer.

SIMPLY SPEAKING

*The greater and more persistent your confidence
in God, the more abundantly you will receive
all that you ask.*

ALBERT THE GREAT

☺ LIVING THE GOD LIFE

What requests do you have for which you need to "ask," "seek," or "knock"? Be persistent in your prayers—the answer will be worth the wait!

REJOICE IN THE LORD.

Rejoice in the Lord always. I will say it again: Rejoice!

PHILIPPIANS 4:4

Sitting in a primitive jail cell in Ephesus—a city in present-day Turkey—Paul began writing a thank-you note to the members of the church in Philippi. The recipients, seeing that God was using the great missionary and apostle in a unique way, had sent him a generous financial gift, which brought him great encouragement. But what encouragement could Paul impart back to them? They were free, yet he was imprisoned for his faith. What could he offer the Philippians from a prison cell?

One thought then came to mind that held great meaning to him during his captivity in prison: rejoice in the Lord.

Cynicism, negativity, and complaining often imprison us during our episodes of mistreatment and misunderstanding. Yet those reactions restrict us from growing closer to God because they reflect our disbelief in His goodness, faithfulness, and desire to walk us through our pain.

Rejoicing in the Lord, on the other hand, means to be joyful in God. Interestingly enough, the Bible usually refers to rejoicing in the context of pain. Rejoicing in the Lord releases us to grow closer to God because through it we communicate to Him our belief in His presence right in the middle of our pain.

Rejoicing should not be equated with denial. Denial refuses to acknowledge the reality of our situation. Rejoicing in the Lord, however, shifts the focus from our pain to God's character. It's honest about the pain, but also honest about God's goodness and love.

Whenever you struggle with cynicism, negativity, or complaining, make the decision to be joyful. Don't focus on your problems (or the people behind the problems), focus on the Problem-Solver: God. Rejoice in the Lord!

SIMPLY SPEAKING

Life need not be easy to be joyful. Joy is not the absence of trouble but the presence of Christ.

WILLIAM VAN DER HOVEN

☺ LIVING THE GOD LIFE

Why not write a psalm of joy to the Lord today?

KEEP A JOURNAL.

We continually remember before our God and Father your work produced by faith, your labor prompted by love, and your endurance inspired by hope in our Lord Jesus Christ.

1 THESSALONIANS 1:3

In the course of your spiritual journey to know God better, you will have many experiences, some joyous adventures in faith, others deep, dark nights of the soul when you struggle with pain and adversity. There will be the moments of quiet reflection and the "Aha!" insights gleaned from the Word and prayer. These moments are the fabric of your life in God, and you won't want to trust them to memory alone. Record them in a journal, and you will create a spiritual treasure that will bless and encourage you all along the way.

The best choice for this type of journal is a simple spiral notebook that lays flat and can be slipped into your Bible or easily carried with you. For each entry, record the date, then the Scripture you're studying, the specific prayer you're praying, a few details to jog your memory later, and any insights the Lord gives you that day. Write down what the Lord is saying to your heart, whether it takes two pages or two lines. Writing will help you remember later, but it will also help you assimilate the insights God is giving you.

Of course, the journaling won't be effective if you never stop to read it again. On those days when you can't seem to hear from God, nothing seems new or fresh, or your problems are bearing down on you, stunting your spiritual progress, open it up and read all the wonderful and exciting things God has shown you and done for you in the past. Soon you'll feel yourself growing closer again.

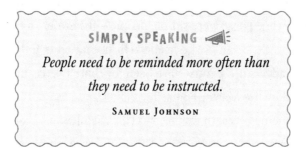

SIMPLY SPEAKING

People need to be reminded more often than they need to be instructed.

SAMUEL JOHNSON

☺ LIVING THE GOD LIFE

Why not start a prayer journal to record all of the wonderful answers God sends and the miracles He provides? When you look back years from now, you will be amazed to recall all of the incredible blessings God has showered upon your life.

BECOME A PRESENT-DAY DISCIPLE.

*[Jesus said,] Whoever serves me must follow me; and where I am, my
servant also will be. My Father will honor the one who serves me.*

JOHN 12:26

When Jesus was ready to begin His earthly ministry, He
chose twelve disciples who walked with Him throughout the
Galilean countryside, watching, learning, and imitating the
things He did. These were simple people—fishermen, a tax
collector, a physician—who heeded His invitation to follow.
What an adventure it must have been for those twelve, being
mentored by the Master Himself.

Jesus' time on earth was brief—His disciples spent a mere
three years with Him. However, His ministry continues to this
day through the power of the Holy Spirit. For that reason, you
have the opportunity to become a disciple as well, walking in
close fellowship with the Master.

This will mean changes in your life. Like all those who
followed Jesus, you will be asked to leave much behind. That
could mean giving up friends who may draw you away from
your godly adventure. It could mean abandoning old habits
and patterns of thinking. It could mean getting rid of some
of the superficial spiritual clutter in your life in order to

make room for the exercise of true godliness.

Discipleship comes with a hefty price tag, but the payoff is more precious than anything you could acquire on earth. A close, personal relationship with God is an adventure so amazing that you will never consider turning back to your old life. Jesus is calling, "Come, follow Me." Will you follow?

SIMPLY SPEAKING 📢

Jesus Christ always talked about discipleship with an "if." We are at perfect liberty to toss our spiritual head and say, "No, thank you, that is a bit too stern for me," and the Lord will never say a word, we can do exactly what we like. He will never plead, but the opportunity is there, "If. . . ."

OSWALD CHAMBERS

😊 LIVING THE GOD LIFE

In what ways have you been following the Master as His disciple? In what ways do you need to follow Him more?

SET YOUR SIGHTS ON HEAVEN—AND NEVER LOOK BACK.

The Spirit of God . . . puts a little of heaven in our hearts so that we'll never settle for less.

2 CORINTHIANS 5:5 MSG

Our homes say a lot about us. They reveal our values, our priorities, our fears. Most people spend a great deal of time and energy creating homes they will enjoy for years to come.

If you set your sights on your earthly home, then you'll be concerned about creating a life of security and comfort. You'll invest your time in what brings you the greatest amount of pleasure. And anything that disrupts or destroys any part of your home will bring your world crashing down.

But if your home is in heaven, then your priorities will look much different. Security, comfort, and pleasure may come and go, but they no longer serve as values that drive your life. Disruptions and destruction may affect you, even rattle you, but your world won't come crashing down because this world is not your home.

Great men and women of faith in the Bible experienced tremendous hardship and difficulty. Some endured famine; some, enormous personal loss. Others suffered severe deprivation and violent persecution for their faith in Christ. But what helped them make it through the hard times was their understanding of where their real home was.

If you want to grow closer to God, invest in your future home. Align your priorities so they reflect God's. Don't make security, comfort, and pleasure in this world your chief concerns, because you can't take them into the next life and this life is short compared with eternity.

Jesus has already prepared a home for you. So set your sights on heaven. Live with eternity on your mind and never look back.

SIMPLY SPEAKING

I will not just live my life. I will not just spend my life. I will invest my life.

HELEN KELLER

☺ LIVING THE GOD LIFE

What can you do today that will be an investment in your future heavenly home?